Home-spun Schools

Also by Dr. Raymond S. Moore

Home-Grown Kids (with Dorothy Moore)
School Can Wait
Better Late Than Early
Science Discovers God
China Doctor
Michibiki: The Leading of God
A Guide to Higher Education Consortiums
Consortiums in American Higher Education

Home-spun Schools

Teaching Children at Home— What Parents Are Doing and How They Are Doing It

Raymond & Dorothy Moore

WITH PENNY ESTES WHEELER AND HOME SCHOOL PARENTS

WORD BOOKS
PUBLISHER
WACO, TEXAS

A DIVISION OF
WORD, INCORPORATED

Library of Congress catalog card number: 82–50843
Printed in the United States of America

To our parents
and our children
and to all families
who make the home first

Contents

ONE

Home-Spun Schools

Meg Johnson, a New Jersey mother, tells it about as well as anyone we have heard. She says, "I can't see why I should give up my children at five or six to be reared by others just when they are the most fun. And when you add to that the support of research, and the risks in many of today's schools, it does not leave Doug and me any choice." She had just delivered her fourth child at this writing.

"For us," she adds, "home school is the perfect answer."

We surprise many people when we suggest that the home, not the school, was the original educational system. The school, not the home, is the substitute. Until the last century, most children who went to school started at twelve or later. Nor has mass education proven itself as much as many of us have hoped. In fact, it is being most seriously questioned. And, *where possible*, parents are more and more often opting for the home. So the home-spun school has become the fastest developing educational movement in America—now perhaps exceeding a quarter of a million students—and once again proving its worth as an original.

For most parents, like the Johnsons, family schools do not so much wage war against regular schools as they shelter little children from what Cornell's Urie Bronfenbrenner calls the "social

9

contagion" of our age—the habits, manners, gestures, vulgarities, obscenities, deceptions, ridicule, and rivalry rampant among school children today. We do not recommend home schools for fainthearted mothers and fathers who are more concerned about social pressures than the future of their children. Rather, it is our goal to build wise, courageous parents who love their children, and strong institutions to which most youngsters will one day go.

To take little children unnecessarily out of the home and put them into institutions—preschool, kindergarten, formal school—before they are ready is perhaps our most pervasive form of child abuse today. As a number of leading psychologists and psychiatrists point out, the child who feels rejected is usually more damaged than the one who is physically bruised. And no matter how we rationalize—that "our children want to go to school" or "everybody is doing it"—the child usually senses rejection when put out of the nest before he is "ready to fly."

The attitude of parents is crucial in the home school. After that comes the question of ability to teach. History records the excellence of parents as teachers, and the genius of their pupils— Melanchthon, John Quincy Adams, William Penn, Abraham Lincoln and Franklin Roosevelt, among thousands. The home school has produced far more than its share of these great leaders. If the mother and father are reasonably warm, responsive and consistent, it matters little whether they have a teaching certificate or college degree. Some of the most spectacular home-school successes have come with parents who have no more than a high-school education.

"But suppose they don't know English or math?" a local schoolman asked my wife and me the other day.

"Most of them," we replied, "have at least enough to satisfy state standards." I had been a public school superintendent, too. And Dorothy is a very specialized remedial-reading teacher.

He shook his head wonderingly.

"How about us teachers?" we countered. "How much do we really know?" We referred to recent findings in Texas and elsewhere that fully half of the teacher applicants scored lower in math than the average high-school junior, and a third scored lower in English. And personality ratings were deplorable. We also recalled the statement of former University of Chicago professor Don Erickson that a teaching certificate does not guarantee good teaching.

This time he shook his head knowingly.

"We've lost a lot of ground," he groaned. "We have a rough road ahead."

He was a good educator, but an embarrassed one. We reflected for a while on the kind of reasoning by our state of Michigan that requires every normal child to be in school by age six, yet winks at the twelve-year-old handicapped child up the road whose Down's Syndrome demands much more knowledgeable effort than does any normal child. He stays home with impunity!

"It really *is* astonishing," he admitted, "that the State requires parents to give up the children which are the most easily taught." We all agreed that it was a slap in the parent's face to suggest that the State could out-parent most mothers and fathers.

There are many beautiful teachers, men and women alike— warm, thoughtful, very special models for our kids. But not even the best of them can do as much all day for a normal child in his class of twenty or thirty or forty peers, as a reasonably loving and consistent parent can do on a one-to-one basis in an hour and a half to two hours at home.

Unless and until we give our children informal opportunities *whenever possible* to develop backgrounds for learning to which they can later attach formal school facts, until we give their learning tools time to be tempered, and until we allow time for their value systems to be stabilized—so as to avoid much of today's peer dependency—our schools will not be able to function efficiently, simply because their grist is not yet ripe and ready for the school mill.

If on the other hand this is not possible, because of physical or financial or psychological problems, and the school is the best environment, then send the child to school, but strive to keep the school program informal until at least 8 to 10. Sometimes a mother finds, for example, that she has a personality clash with one of her children. Still other parents simply don't have the will to cope with their youngsters; this is sad, but such children may be much better off in a school—depending, of course, on the school.

The main things to remember here are (1) that ideally the home is the first and finest educational nest (the school, at least until 8 to 10 or 12, is at best a substitute for the home); and (2) when we give our schools children whose minds and values are ready, they will usually turn out children who are academic, behavioral and social leaders. We need these leaders badly today.

The stories that follow in this book are typical of the thousands of home-school parents who have called, written or visited us. Nearly every one has proven to be an above-average teacher. Yet they were not selected so much because their children achieved so well, as to demonstrate that home schools work well under almost any kind of circumstance. They do well in city or country, among rich or poor, professional or blue collar, married or single parents, whether educated in high school or college, in the U.S. or overseas.

Recipe for home-school teaching. The requirements are not complex. Parents need only be loving, responsive, and reasonably consistent, and salt these qualities with a little imagination, common sense, and willingness to follow a few simple suggestions in this book.* And don't worry about the opinions of neighbors who don't know or care about the real needs of children. Just be kind to them. Have your children be helpful in your home and in the neighborhood. Visit the old and infirm and ill. Do favors for others without asking any in return. Soon your "strange antics" will be forgotten . . . or admired.

In one sense you are teaching all your waking moments—as models to your offspring. Yet while some parents are more dili-

---

*And in *Home-Grown Kids* (Waco, TX: Word Books, Publisher), 1981.

gent than others, none need to formally teach a full school day. Seldom are more than two or three hours of formal academic instruction a day appropriate. Many mothers and fathers limit their formal teaching to little more than an hour. Some form family corporations and make, sell, and earn.

Much more important is your working with your children in physical work, helping them learn practical skills and the nobility of work—building character qualities of initiative, industry, neatness, order, responsibility, and dependability, which are hard to find in even one in ten children or young adults today.

Along with these grosser values you can by precept and example teach manners and graces which today are rare—kindness, thoughtfulness, tact, forgiveness, generosity, and a just plain kind of for-others love. This is seldom done in schools these days. Teach them how to walk tall, how to listen closely, how to speak graciously. Paul was not gesturing idly when he wrote Philippians 4:8, "Finally, brethren, whatsoever things are true, whatsoever things are pure, whatsoever things are lovely, whatsoever things are of good report; . . . think on these things." This is also a good guide to book selection.

With this kind of teaching, accompanied by well-regulated physical work in fellowship with you, comes also a moral tone which is not otherwise possible. A sound work-study program is a key to moral purity. It teaches self-worth, which in turn is the principal dynamic of positive sociability and is also crucial in fulfilling today's need for racial understanding. If you follow such a simple routine and use materials from any of a number of excellent sources (see Appendix A), your children will excel academically. But this is not all. Their behavior will be superior too! And socially they will generally be outstanding.

Typically today in schools, children are fed along with their studies a narcissistic, me-first mixture of busing, sports, amusements, and snacks—empty-calorie food mentally, physically and spiritually. Why shouldn't they instead learn an altruistic, my-neighbor-first mixture of work and service and joy of sharing? No matter the religion, from Christianity or Judaism to Confucianism and from Taoism or Islam to Zen, the golden rule threads through them all. And the home is its finest nest. It is the person who understands this well who is the most able creator of a family school.

In all this there are some simple child-development concepts which every home-school parent should understand. These ideas may seem new to some because they are so different from conventional practice. But they are actually quite old-fashioned, and neatly blend research and common sense. *

Our early childhood and home-school research grew out of experiences in the classroom with children who were misbehaving or not learning—largely because they were not ready for formal schooling. We set out to determine the best ages for school entrance, concerned first with *academic achievement.* Yet more important has become the *socialization* of young children— which also addresses senses, coordination, brain development, reason and social-emotional aspects of child development. These conclusions come from our Stanford, University of Colorado Medical School, Michigan State and Hewitt investigative teams who did basic research and analyzed more than seven thousand early childhood studies. We offer briefly here our conclusions which we would like to have you check against any sound research that you know. Note how sociality depends as much on the child's maturity as do his studies. And even more on his environment!

Readiness for learning. Despite early excitement for school, most early entrants (ages four, five, six, etc.) are tired from school pressures before they are out of the third or fourth grades—at about the ages and levels we found that they should be starting. Noted Piagetian psychologist David Elkind says these youngsters are "burned out." They would have been far better off

---

Home-Spun Schools and its companion book, *Home-Grown Kids,* will shortly be followed by a parent-child series of little "How-we-did-it-down-our-street" books on How to Be Kind, How to Obey, How to Work, How to Have Good Manners, How to Be Safe, How to Walk, etc., tentatively titled "The Mystery Kids" series.

wherever possible waiting until ages eight to ten or later to start formal studies (at home or school) in the second, third, fourth or fifth grade. They would then quickly pass early entrants in learning, behavior and sociability. Their vision, hearing and other senses are not ready for continuing formal programs of learning until age eight or nine. (Maturity may vary three or four years during this preteen period.) When earlier care is absolutely necessary, it should be informal, warm and responsive—like a good home—with a low adult-to-child ratio. Some top psychologists suggest that age twelve to fourteen would be ideal.

The eyes of most children are permanently damaged by too much close work before age twelve. Neither the maturity of their delicate central nervous systems nor the "balancing" of the hemispheres of their brains, nor yet the insulation of their nerve pathways provide a basis for thoughtful learning before eight or nine. They have little understanding of certain basic concepts which are part and parcel of thoughtful formal learning—such as time, speed, weight, space, distance, and direction. And their reaction time is much slower than most adults expect. The *integration* of these *maturity levels* (IML)—brain, reason, hearing, vision, taste, touch, smell, coordination, etc., comes for most between eight and ten or twelve.

Our findings coincide with the well-established conclusions of Jean Piaget and others that children cannot handle cause-and-effect reasoning in any consistent way before late sevens to middle elevens. They have a hard time answering "Why?" and "How?" They are unable to correctly and consistently judge motives. The fives and sixes are usually subjected to dull Dick and Jane rote learning which tires, frustrates and ruins motivation, requires little thought, stimulates few "hows" and "whys." Net results: frequent learning failure, delinquency, and mental illness. For example, little boys trail little girls about a year in maturity, yet are unfairly under the same school entrance laws. So HEW figures show that learning failure and delinquency hits three or four boys for every girl, and boys are at least four times more likely to be acutely hyperactive. So unknowing teachers far more often tag little boys as "naughty" or "dumb." These labels frequently follow them through school. *And the bright child is no exception;* in fact, because of his native "quickness" he may go much faster in the wrong direction.

Socialization. We later found that little children are not only better taught at home than at school, but are also better socialized by parental example and sharing than by other little children. This idea was fed by many researchers. Among the more prominent were Dr. Bronfenbrenner who found that up to the sixth grade at least, children who spend more of their elective time with their peers than their parents tend to become peer dependent; and Stanford's Albert Bandura and others who noted that this tendency has in recent years moved down to preschool levels—*which should be avoided whenever good parenting is possible.* Contrary to common beliefs, then, little children are not best socialized by other kids, and socialization is not neutral. It is either positive or negative.

(1) *Positive,* or altruistic and principled, sociability is firmly linked with the family—with the quantity and quality of self-worth. This is in turn dependent largely on the track of values and experience provided by the family *at least* until the child can reason consistently. In other words, the child who works and eats and plays and has his rest and is read to daily, more with his parents than with his peers, senses that he is part of the family corporation—needed, wanted, depended upon. He is the one who has a sense of self-worth. And when he does enter school, preferably not before eight to ten, he usually becomes a social leader. He knows where he is going, is self-directed and independent in values and skills. He largely avoids the dismal pitfalls and social cancer of peer dependency. He is the *productive* citizen our nation badly needs.

Thus, home-school youngsters are not in social straitjackets. They generally are outgoing, well-socialized examples of modern youth. Visit Brigid Horbinski's girls in Marietta, Georgia—well-poised examples of preteen hostesses. Or call on Donna Brinkle's boys in Oveido, Florida. Donna has home-taught them through high school, and the results are impressive. Watch Mark Schaefer as he helps in the pediatric ward of a local California medical center. Or visit the Virgil Longs in West Point, Nebraska or the Darrell Ownbys of Rolla, Missouri, and revel in beautiful, thoughtful children. The NEA should take a look!

(2) *Negative*, me-first sociability, on the other hand, is born from too great a proportion of peer-group association and too few meaningful parental contacts and responsibility experiences in the home during the first eight to twelve years. The early peer influence generally brings an indifference to family values which defy parent correction. The child does not yet consistently understand the "why" of parental demands when his peers replace his parents as his models because he is with them more. So he does what comes naturally: he adapts to the ways of his agemates because "everybody's doing it," and gives his parent's values the back of his little hand. And . . . he has few sound values to pass on to the next generation. He is seldom truly practical, productive, self-directed, or patriotic.

Here are the makings of the rebels of the sixties, the drug and sex culture of the seventies and the perverse society of the eighties. On the other hand, we have never yet found a drug fix in a home school. Home schoolers usually have a keen sense of direction and are social leaders in their neighborhoods. Their homes are often social centers for the kids who instinctively know which parents care.

So home, wherever possible, is by far the best nest until at least eight to ten. Where there is any reasonable doubt about the influence of schools on our children (morality, ridicule, rivalry, denial of religious values, etc.) home schools are usually a highly desirable alternative. At least 34 states permit them by law under various conditions. Other states permit them through court decisions. Yet some which do not permit them by law are actually more lenient than some of those who do.

Most educators still are more concerned for the welfare of children than the letter of the law. And they should be. Home schools nearly always excel regular schools in achievement. And although most parents don't know it, they are clearly the best teachers of their own children at least through ages ten to twelve. And if they don't do this, their children usually suffer.

To the credit of many legislatures and public school educators, many state policies are often understanding of the child's needs and alert to the parents' constitutional rights. Often, however, these policies are not adequately communicated to the county and local school districts. As a result, we have had many parents called to account in such states as Maryland, Missouri and California where state policies are lenient. We had three such cases from Missouri in one week. When we referred them to the chief state attendance officer, he quickly called the school districts and interceded for the parents.

In some states, such as Colorado and New York, present school officials interpret otherwise rigid laws in favor of parents. In Nebraska and Illinois, among others, the courts have liberally interpreted for home schools. And Alaska and Louisiana have led the way in actually changing the laws to provide for parental priorities. State legislator Louis "Woody" Jenkins wrote a model for the nation in his Louisiana law. And he credits one mother, Hazel Anderson, for keeping at him until he carried it through.

Often our phone rings with calls from parents who badly want to start home schools but have little confidence in their ability to teach. We educators have done a colossal job of brainwashing them into thinking we can out-parent them. Even the University of Chicago's Benjamin Bloom, whose research helped make early schooling a popular trend in this country, now admits that parents are the best teachers, and that they can be educated as teachers in the home. With a little help, a mother or father can relax and quickly get used to the program, shaping it around their family.

Yet there are some ideas which apply generally to all home-school beginners. We might call them "The Ten Little Commandments for Home Schools." They come from the personal experiences of men and women, from such home-school specialists as John Holt of Boston; Patty Blankenship of Atlanta; the

Roland Morrows of Central City, Nebraska; Meg Johnson and Nancy Plent of New Jersey; Donna Brinkle of Florida; the Bergmans of Smithton, Missouri; Ed Nagel of Santa Fe, New Mexico; and from our experiences with thousands of home-school families. Supporters vary from such constitutional experts as Leo Pfeffer of New York City and such leading defense lawyers as William Ball of Harrisburg, Pennsylvania; John Whitehead of Washington, D.C.; and David Gibbs, Charles Craze and Milt Schulman of Cleveland, Ohio; to such prosecutors as Dale Ruohomaki of Marquette, Michigan; and John Cooley of Napa, California. *

1. Be sure of your beliefs and goals as parents; decide if the needs of your children are more important to you than social pressures and bad laws, and if you can be a compassionate neighbor when others think you strange. The more you know about your children, the more likely you will cope.

2. Examine your willingness to be a patient, warm, responsive and consistent parent. If you can't handle your children, learn how, like the parents in this book have done. Otherwise put them in a good school or farm them out to someone who *can* guide them.

3. Learn how your children develop so that you can talk knowledgeably and with assurance to your school officials. We have prepared such books as *Home-Grown Kids, Better Late Than Early* and *School Can Wait* to help you.

4. Learn your rights as parents. You will find considerable information in this book. More will be gleaned from such books as *Home-Grown Kids* or from home school centers. (See Appendix A).

5. Seek the best counsel available, usually through your center. But if necessary, reach out to national specialists and don't go into court without experienced counsel and witnesses.

6. Settle on a curriculum compatible with your ability and beliefs (Appendix A). Many parents later find that they can build their own courses of study without helper schools, but experienced suppliers are a good bet when you begin.

7. Keep a balance in your program. Don't tie yourself down to

books all day. An hour and a half to two hours is ample time for formal education in a typical home school. No formal education at all is needed before age eight or ten. But work, read, sing, play, rest, eat and go places with your children. If you have more than one child, use the older to teach the younger and the stronger to help the weaker. Home school should be less perplexity than fun. You are teaching by example every moment. Respond warmly. Use your imagination. Everything within sight, sound, touch, taste and smell is a learning tool.

8. Don't make a big thing out of being different, but don't be ashamed either. Name your home school, so that when asked, your children can say, like Corinne Johnson (Chapter 3), "Yes, I go to "Sunrise," or like Leslie Sue Rice (Chapter 5), "I go to the Rice Christian Academy." It may be wise to consider yourself a branch of your supplier school (Appendix A), or set up as a satellite of a local public, private or parochial school, or you may arrange for supervision by a certified teacher if you must have the confidence of local school officials. Remember, no two home schools will be exactly alike. If you are determined to meet the needs of your child, you will do very well.

9. Most school officials seem to prefer that you move ahead quietly, although in states like California you usually file an affidavit with your state or county school office. If officials challenge you or threaten arrest, be calm, offer evidence of the rightness of your doings, ask if in face of your evidence they have any better ideas.* If they are persistent, seek specialists' help. There are usually many recourses short of court, such as injunction, hearings with boards of education, and reasoning by specialists on your behalf with officials—which often quickly settles the case. For parents of faith this also means prayer.

10. Keep your cool. If your children do not learn as fast as you think they should, take counsel. Be patient. Note Marge

---

*Many parents have successfully used *Home Grown Kids* or *School Can Wait* or *Better Late Than Early* by the authors.

Schaefer's fears in Chapter 2—about her middle son reading little at age nine, but reading like an adult six months later— when he was ready. It is seldom good to rush music lessons or gymnastics or other popular skills. Most music teachers say it is best not to start lessons before age eleven. When lessons are begun too early, children often want to shift expensively from instrument to instrument or tire of music lessons altogether. A child's excitement for early music lessons is seldom mature. And parental pressures on an unready child can lead to calamity. A potential prodigy need not also be a neurotic.

It is dangerously past time for parents to learn of their astonishing privileges of rearing children, and also to know their rights—which are constitutionally guaranteed. Our citizenship privileges will not long be worth the paper they are written on if we do not support those parents who are principled enough to put their children ahead of the selfish pressures of vested interests. We must challenge reckless states and their local agents—the few social workers and schoolmen who still persecute conscientious, capable mothers and fathers.

Remember, when you surrender your parental authority and responsibility to the state, you are still accountable for your children, but you never fully retrieve your authority. Be careful, thoughtful and fully informed before you give away your own, lest you like others pay a price in damaged children.

If we are to believe such eminent sociologists as Frederick Le Play, J. D. Unwin or Carle Zimmerman, we must spend more time with our children in the home and protect them from decadent pressures and laws lest our society collapse like that of Greece or Rome, when their societies' conditions were virtually identical to ours.

Let's have more warmth and consistent firmness, less indulgence; more work *with you,* more tools, sticks, nails than fancy toys; more service for others—the old, the young, the poor, the infirm—and less sports and amusements; more self-control, patriotism, productiveness and responsibility—which lead to, and follow, self-worth as noble citizens. Parents and home, un-diluted, usually do this best.

Then help other parents. Form or join a home-school support group if possible. Associate *actively* with your local or state home school groups, and keep up to date by reading such papers as the Hewitt *Family Report* (see Appendix A). Watch your state legislation closely. Ask your local legislator to keep you informed. Your voice has power only when it is heard with full information.

TWO

The Nurse and the PR Man
——————————with Marge Schaefer——————————

I was scared that I was losing my son. The surety, the absolute certainty of that fact lay heavy on my mind, spreading like a dark stain, tingeing every thought with despair.

I hardly knew him, Mark, my firstborn. Always on the quiet side, now sullenness clouded his expression. He'd built a wall about himself, topped it with barbed wire and withdrawn behind it where the kids couldn't hurt him anymore. Yet the same barrier that protected him from the jibes and put-downs of his peers separated him from us, his parents. Our love, our concern bounced off Mark's wall, his face a closed door we could not enter.

We were desperate.

Mark was in the fourth grade and in a church school.

The trouble had been brewing for years, smoldering. It affected all of our lives. Mark's younger brothers became the target for all the anger he feared to direct at his classmates. Home emerged as a battleground for all the skirmishes Mark lost at school.

"Burning each other" they called it . . . the slamming, the taunting, the cruel jokes. The bigger guys picked on the smaller. The stronger on the weak. And the weak in turn found someone weaker to "burn" and the chain continued. It goes on all the

23

time. But few parents either seemed to know or care enough to do something about it. We had to.

An older boy riding in Mark's car pool kept his life miserable. "Cool man of the group," his reputation, with the proper swagger and the perfect verbal razor thrusts. Day after day Mark endured his teasing—afraid, unable to meet him on his own turf—becoming more and more withdrawn. Home, he turned on his brothers. Jonathan and Jeffery became victims of the pecking order.

Yet this was only one section of the jigsaw.

The whole school situation concerned me. Mean little tricks were the rule of the day, such as pulling chairs out from under a person about to sit down and loud laughter when he fell. An old joke, never very funny. Flushing shoes, sweaters, anything to stop up the toilets. And what rivalry! Always and forever competing to be the biggest, the strongest, the best. Dirty words written and rewritten on walls and the smirks about them that followed.

"But you can't protect your kids from everything," people said. "Life is rough. Sometimes kids are foolish, even cruel."

No, I'd think. I never even tried to protect my sons from everything. But this is too much. The pressure is too great. There are too many dangerous jokes. The bathroom floor has been awash with a toilet's overflow much too often. Too many kids are being hurt by too many slashing put-downs. Mark is withdrawing . . . from them and from us. He's being burned beyond what he can endure. If you think this is an exaggeration, you are starkly naïve, badly unaware or poorly informed.

How many times can you be killed by words?

We decided to take Mark out of school. Not a snap decision, but one born of frustration, then desperation. Once decided, it seemed the logical solution. So simple we wondered why we hadn't thought of it before.

Mark was agreeable, even relieved. So we simply went to the principal and told him Mark was withdrawing. The man didn't understand. Perhaps he couldn't understand. Surely he hadn't seen or lived with our pain. He said we were foolish, we were fanatical. He said that we couldn't possibly offer our children the resources that the school had. If everybody did what we were doing there'd be a bunch of fruits running around.

His words ping-ponged against us, a torrent, but we hardly felt them. There were some implied threats that we would be reported. I had no doubts at this point. Too many hours had I begged God for an answer, for the way to save our family. I no longer felt uncertain or insecure.

We were able to buy Mark's schoolbooks and would continue with the subjects he had in the classroom.

I called a local church pastor and asked if he knew of someone we could contact to supervise Mark's work. Though I'm a registered nurse, I, like any typical parent, felt incapable of guiding his study. The pastor put us in touch with a certified teacher. For the remainder of that first year of home school, we met with her once a week. Observing her guidance, by the next school year I felt enough confidence in myself and in Mark to let him work without her.

We were not without problems, however.

We were reported to the local authorities. Our regional church officer of education sent me a letter outlining the legal implications of what we were doing. He wished us success and gave me a catalog of books I could order, but in actuality gave us no support or encouragement at all.

We felt the pressure and I was tempted to cave in under it. No matter whether you like to admit it or not, what other people think of you is important. Then we made a decision—a wise decision—to go to the local school system itself and talk with the attendance officer. We would do our own reporting.

I might confess that at this point my courage wasn't any too great, but the man was very understanding. He told me there would be no problem as long as our home program was monitored by a certified teacher from the district.

We wrote a summary of our reasons for removing Mark from school and gave them a list of the books we'd be using and the curriculum. We did the same the following September when Mark began home study again and sent it to the local school officer in charge of attendance.

As it turned out, our program was so successful that after a few months they didn't concern themselves with us any more.

Our next-door neighbor, herself the principal of a local public school, supported us from the beginning and, in fact, still does. She became a liaison between us and school authorities and they have not contacted us since.

After the first year our home school evolved into something quite different from that of a normal classroom. As our concept of education has changed to include the *whole* person, our curricula changed also.

The boys—now ages fifteen, twelve, and eleven—study the three R's, plus Bible, English, spelling, science, music and typing.

We avoid "grading" as much as possible. Mark is in the ninth grade, so his high school textbooks and program differ considerably from his brothers. Jonathan works on the fourth- to eighth-grade levels. Jeffery is a strong fifth-grader but reads on the eighth-grade level. We encourage them to work at their own speed, advancing when they can, and spending extra time on areas in which they are weak.

Our main source of textbooks is Rod and Staff Publishers in Crockett, Kentucky, at a present cost of about sixty dollars per year per child. We appreciate the moral and spiritual emphasis in all subjects published by this company.

Our curricula now fall under four headings: study of Scripture, study of nature, useful labor and experiences of life.

We begin our days with family devotions. The boys study from a Bible textbook and workbook. Then we—the boys and I together—plan their schoolwork for the day. Sometimes they spend two hours on math or reading, depending upon their problems or needs. Other mornings they work in all their textbooks. And some days their projects do not include books at all.

By noon the boys have usually finished their schoolwork and

have the day free for other activities. This is one reason they enjoy home study so much.

They use science textbooks but we find that many other activities teach principles of science through experience: hiking, backpacking in our nearby mountains, for example, and observing the trees and flowers, the rock formations, the birds and insects along the trails. Their pets include birds, horses, rabbits and a tree squirrel. All these require, and to these the boys give, daily attention.

Dick's job takes him as a speaker and representative of his firm to meetings in different areas of the United States and Canada. We travel with him and all enjoy and learn from visiting so many different places.

Mark is responsible for maintaining our cars, checking the levels of oil and water, for example.

One day a week he is a volunteer worker in the pediatrics department of our local hospital. Our once painfully shy and withdrawn fourth-grader now answers the phone, runs errands and supervises the playroom for children who are hospitalized but are unable to walk around and play together.

All the boys work regularly for our neighbors, chosen over the other young men in the area. Of course this makes us happy, but the real benefit is to the boys. There are three public-school teachers on our block and the success of our home program is borne out by the confidence these people have in them. Just recently one told Dick, "No other parents care about their kids like I've seen you people care about yours. I feel there's something stable here that America is losing."

A few months ago Mark began working with his uncle roofing and leveling mobile homes. This job has drawn him out socially as he goes to mobile-home parks, and meets and talks with homeowners. Earning a bit of money, he has his own bank account and takes care of his own expenses, even to buying his clothes.

The three boys are our church's custodians and Mark is the youth representative on our church board. In sharing this with you, I don't mean to imply that no child left in regular school can't do as well as those who study at home. But for us, in our situation, home study has been more than a solution. It's been a blessing to our family.

Mark is still rather quiet. Sometimes he has the very typical adolescent low self-image. But he's level-headed, he's dependable. He's learned self-discipline through studying on his own. His self-confidence has grown and he's tuned into people. Maybe all the pain of his early school years has given him an awareness of other's needs.

The kids love their horses. Jonathan—our most aggressive son—has learned to channel his energies without hurting others. We hardly believed him when he said he planned to build a corral for his pony, but he believed in himself and got busy.

How long does it take a boy to build a corral? How many hours of digging? How many sweat-soaked shirts? How many shovelfuls of dirt? He did it almost single-handedly—sawing, hammering, digging, measuring.

We wondered if he'd stick with it. Surely he'd tire long before this corral became a reality. Probably it would eventually fall down and have to be carted away.

Of course we didn't say this aloud, but wondered if he hadn't started something too big for him to finish. But our young fighter kept at his self-imposed labor. And eight months and countless laboring hours after beginning, Jonathan's pony had a new corral.

But then, Jonathan has always been one to surprise us. Of all the boys, he wanted to begin school the most. We'd already taken Mark out and were so pleased with his progress that we planned to begin Jon at home too. But he begged. School. Desks. Lots and lots of children and a real teacher. We gave in and enrolled him in the first grade.

He didn't last long.

After three months of increasing hyperactivity his teacher told us, "He's like a little caged animal. It's not right to force him to remain." He could not handle the confines and rigidity of the classroom schedule. We took him out and eventually began teaching him at home. How many are there like him?

We had another problem with Jonathan. Of course, he didn't see it that way. To him it was *our* problem, not his. *Jon didn't want to learn to read.*

He's always been a bit immature for his age, but nine years old! A nine-year-old kid running around, not reading! Not able to read. Not interested. Dr. Raymond Moore had told me that some boys don't read until ten or later, but this was *my* boy. Besides, I am not the most patient person in the world, and I began to get worried. There are all those people out there—the church school principal, the critical neighbor, just waiting for a failure!

I mean, it's one thing to teach your children at home. Our friends and relatives have grown used to that idea. But letting Jonathan run around free as a lamb—or really more like a colt— and not reading? Impossible!

So I decided to teach him. We sat down together. We looked at bright pictures and large-print first-grade words. He couldn't have cared less. I began to push, push hard. I began to feel frantic inside. War developed between me and my middle son. I pushed harder, but he planted his feet and refused to budge.

Can you *force* anybody to learn?

To make matters worse my husband intervened and not in my favor. "Back off," he suggested. "You may have the kid under more pressure than he'd get at school."

"But he won't learn to read. He simply refuses."

Dick smiled patiently. "He's only nine."

Only nine?

"It's not only a matter of years. He's not mature for his age. Let him take care of the animals and travel with us. Can't you let him be a little kid a while longer? You don't force a horse to race before he's ready."

My mouth closed. I tried to keep it that way. After all, Dick was head of the family. But it wasn't easy.

Mark continued to work well alone, under my guidance.

Jonathan went backpacking with us. He did his chores around the house and helped me in the kitchen. He fed the bunnies. Summer came and we began traveling with Dick. A year passed. He still didn't read.

Then—without warning—one day my ears told me something I couldn't believe. "I want to learn to read like Mark because he can read the signs along the freeway." It was Jonathan! And a miracle of maturity.

It was the Fourth of July to me, and Christmas, all in one day!

We bought a child's book with a record, a read-along-while-you-listen device. He played the record. He followed along in his book.

He picked up other books and began to study them. Because he'd long had an interest in Indians, we got him *Friday, the Arapaho,* a two-hundred-page book. Within four months he'd read it from cover to cover about fifteen times. Within six months his oral reading became as accurate and well enunciated as most adults'. Once he started, no one could stop him. I marveled. But I later found for myself that this was not particularly unusual.

Jeffery, our even-tempered eleven-year-old, sometimes expresses the wish to attend a "real" school. This is usually in response to pressure from his friends. Mark and Jon, however, soon talk him out of it by pointing out all the advantages they enjoy.

Jeff is learning how to be strong around kids whose standards and attitudes are different from his. Recently he has realized that he needs to be aware of how others influence him and not to follow the gang unless they're on a wise path.

Despite the fact that he doesn't spend five to six hours a day in a classroom with other kids, Jeff is learning pleasant social skills and social awareness. He converses well with both children and adults. He will be a sound leader.

People ask us how long this will go on. We will keep the kids studying at home as long as they want to and we sense that they are ahead of the learning game. It's possible that Mark and Jonathan might decide to return to regular school before they complete the twelfth grade. We've discussed this with them. If they request this, they understand that we will be very selective, leaning toward a small, rural school with a strong work-study program, a school that emphasizes spiritual and practical living, where teachers work with students.

Our emphasis is not on testing them against the norms. Some norms these days are declining. We prefer instead that they develop their own highest potential.

After completing the requirements of high school they will take the GED test and college entrance exams. We have no doubts about their success.

Yet the greatest reward from our home school is the closeness of our family, the family that we were losing. Instead we are friends.

If "friends" doesn't mean anything to you, maybe it's because you're still fighting your children. Some mothers confess that their kids are the enemy and they don't know how to cope. Others have children who are so wrapped up in a multitude of activities that they become strangers though they sleep under the same roof. I just recently read in a national magazine a mother's statement. Her children grown, she sought work with children to fill the void. "Time passes so fast," she mused. "At age three they go to nursery school. At six they're in first grade. Before you know it they're out of high school and married. Where does time go?"

If I were an artist I'd capture on paper the pictures of my family that live in my mind. I'd use strong lines and vibrant colors to express the energy that flows between us. I'd show my husband working and wrestling with his sons. I'd show our exhaustion and triumph as we top a mountain trail, putting many things aside that we once saw as necessities.

Then I'd draw a whole sequence of pictures, starting with Mark, shoulders hunched, head down to avoid invisible blows. He'd be sitting off by himself, in our family but not of it.

Next I'd line out a pastel chalk of him bent over his books at the kitchen table, his mouth relaxed but his eyes still cautious.

Then an abstract watercolor of Mark flinging himself upon a horse might capture his freedom, the beginning of his feelings of self-worth.

The last pictures must be done in oils—Mark the man, tender with a small child, self-confident on the church board, tired and fulfilled after a day's work under California's hot sun.

Through home school, I have become acquainted with my sons. Oh, I've been frightened and frustrated, angry, uncertain and elated. Sometimes I tried to push too hard. Often I forgot that education is much more than books. But we did it! We're doing it! And it works.

I wish I could write these words in iridescent colors, I wish I could fling my joy like fireworks across the sky.

We did it—we held school at home.

They did it—they keep up with their studies.

They're learning self-discipline. They're not only growing mentally and physically, but emotionally and spiritually as well.

Dick and I did it.

Dick and I taught them.

Dick and I accepted their limitations and encouraged them when they lagged.

You could almost call us teachers.

I know of many mothers who are unable to spend more than an hour a day with their children before and after school, and even then their attention is divided between several different problems. And I am at the same time sad and joyful. Sad for them and joyful for us, for I would be missing something of infinite value if we were in the same trap. The older the boys get, the more of a surprise and delight they've become. Not that they were so bad before, but to see them maturing, changing, their personalities flowering, has almost been like watching God create something wonderful out of ordinary clay. Every day I am thrilled by their progress.

Yet they aren't isolated from their friends who attend regular school. Our home has become the gathering place where the neighborhood kids flock and stay. It seems a natural—there's so much going on at our house.

We have a sense of bonding and comradeship that we now see is rare in most homes. Working together on their school program—and just working together—has drawn us closer. We confide, we share, we have a strong respect for one another. Instead of our going five separate ways, our greatest joy is doing things together.

Children are born. They grow. They leave the family circle to enter school and are influenced by teachers and peers. They graduate, get jobs, marry and move away. And so often their parents never had the opportunity to know them. There were never enough hours in the day to become friends.

We know ourselves fortunate. We know ourselves blessed. For us and our family school, there's no other way.

THREE

The Schoolmarm and the New York Banker

──────────with Meg Johnson──────────

Some might feel that because I am a trained teacher and my husband is a New York banker, we are not typical home-school people. Perhaps not, but I have worked with enough home-school folks to know that family schools have little relationship to the average teacher-education program. There are reasons to believe that some of these education courses might even be a handicap. A loving mother, just by being a good parent, is a far better than average teacher of her own children. And some of the best of them don't even have a full high-school education. But they have a clear idea of what they want their children to be, and set about to get good advice. And their kids are among the best learners of all.

Five years ago we embarked on what to us was an unconventional experience in child-rearing with our decision to educate our children at home. This has not been at all the awesome, demanding chore that many people imagine it to be. Instead, it has become a rewarding and natural part of our home life, enriching us as parents beyond belief. We cherish our home school as our new response to the God-given responsibility we accepted when we became parents.

We spent several years preparing for our adventure, writing and talking with people and organizations everywhere, from here

34

in New Jersey all across the United States. Our needs were simple enough: information and assistance for our planned home school. Perhaps if we'd been easily discouraged or unconvinced of the value of our project we would have given up, because the only concrete response we received in all that time was information on the Calvert School.

So we began with Calvert, since it provided the so-called "equivalent" education required by New Jersey law. Our action is legal in our state and we have always taken care to maintain cordial relations with our cooperative New Jersey school personnel. The Golden Rule, we think, is a sound guide. I have a Master's degree in special education and am certified in both elementary and special education. However, helpful as my training has been in teaching our children, it surely isn't necessary. The overriding need is simply a mother's total commitment to the program. Her attitude and a reasonable self-confidence are important. And there are many good people to help in this. Thousands, like us, have had a great deal of help and encouragement from the books by Raymond and Dorothy Moore.

Our daughters Melissa and Corinne have never attended a regular school, and at ages eight and nine are now studying on the third- and fifth-grade levels. Our classroom is a small room in our basement, although we use the kitchen, our yard, and our piano in the living room for the many other learning activities. Brad, our five-year-old son, also participates in the experiences we share in our home school.

We learned of the Christian Liberty Academy program and used it concurrently with Calvert for three years, for the girls were in different courses and we were somewhat happier with the unique emphasis of the Christian Liberty Academy. We have always included additional material and have become so secure in our home education that we now plan our own program. We use *McGuffey's Eclectic Readers* and have been pleased with Beka Book publications, using them in many subjects. A Lutheran parochial school course from Concordia Publishing House provides for most of our religious study.

In addition to the essential academic subjects, we include basic etiquette, proper speaking habits, music, homemaking, physical education and art. We also go regularly to the local library and attend chapel each week at a private school a few miles away. The children do not "work" all day, but they do fill up most of the time allotted a normal school day. We try to keep a healthy balance between formal school work and practical activities designed to teach the principles and responsibilities important to their total learning experience as homemakers and workers and sound social creatures.

The costs of our home school have varied. We probably spent about two hundred fifty to three hundred dollars per school-age child until this year. Now we can manage a superior program on about $100–$150 per year, not including extras like field trips and expanding our materials. We find garage and book sales are good sources of many materials. We also have learned to deal directly with our publishers for our texts, such as Rod and Staff of Crockett, Kentucky and Beka Books from the Pensacola Christian School in Florida.

For our own protection, we had a professional psychologist independently check the girls' social development and intellectual abilities when they each became six. Although this cost us over two hundred dollars, and has proved to have been unnecessary, it was valuable to us at the time to have outside reliable confirmation of our apparent success with the children. This past spring we gave them the California Achievement Tests they would have received in school. These were provided and graded by the local school. The girls performed from one to seven grade-levels above their own grades, depending on the subjects, and scored well up in the 90th percentile.

We kept our children home for a number of reasons. We felt there were serious drawbacks in the public school system socially, academically and philosophically. With much emphasis being put on special education in today's schools and on making education viable for every citizen (we have no quarrel with this idea), we feel that the child at the higher end of the ability spectrum is often short-changed and unchallenged. Some gifted children do learn in spite of the system, but many more intelligent youngsters are bored and discouraged, eventually either failing or dropping out. This situation also contributes to a lot of other problems.

We were especially concerned about the social development of our children. We had grave concerns about exposing them to such influences as peer-group pressures and what some call "groupthink." It is quite enough to combat TV (ours is now in the attic), movies, music, certain books and advertising. But we were most concerned about the subtle attack on our Christian values and heritage. Sound moral principles are diluted by the wrong kinds of "values clarification," situation ethics, and so-called behavioral modification practiced on children in schools. We did not feel we could surrender the development of our children's minds to a system which differs so much in its philosophy from ours.

But perhaps the most important reason we had for choosing to keep our children home was that as parents we simply were not ready to give them up at age six. They were getting to be fun. I hesitate to call them *wonderful* and *special* and yet they were— and are—to me. They had reached an age where we could relate to and enjoy them as real "little people." Our companionship was at its highest level since they were born. It just didn't seem fair to turn them over to others who could not possibly get the enjoyment which could be ours, and who could not give the one-to-one care we could provide on our own family-values track.

At first we did not know for certain, even with our college backgrounds, that our home-schooling experiment would work out. If it didn't, we figured the children could always go to school. But if we started them in school, and it didn't work out, we weren't sure we could easily pry them out. Sometimes the school officials take a dim view, and sometimes youngsters protest.

Yet, it was for *their* needs and well-being more than our own that we wanted to keep them home at least until age eight or ten. Although they probably would have accepted and adjusted to school, they were willing and content to stay at home. Emotionally, a child needs the strength and security of his family until he is at least eight or ten. And, during this early period, most children are not physically ready—their nervous systems are not sufficiently developed—for the expectations and pressures of school.

In many children, their eyes are not sufficiently developed to thoughtfully "see" what is expected of them over the long period of a school day. For instance, even very intelligent children frequently have little or no ability in these early years to distinguish between a b and a d and a p, or a 3 and a 5, or 6 and 9. These physical immaturities put added stress on the nervous system and the emotions. We had read and observed that school is tiring and upsetting to these very young children. They are often frustrated and anxiety-ridden and are subjected to rivalry and ridicule on the buses and at school. By the time their physical ability catches up with their mental ability, their self-esteem has been battered to the point they often incur considerable emotional damage.

We hoped to spare our children some of these problems by teaching them at home in a lower-stress environment, at least until age ten. By that time they would be much more mature and confident. Their values would be stabilized and they would be a bit more ready to meet the world alone.

Not that we haven't had some problems in our own little school. Though Corinne has had little difficulties in her studies, she has had a hard time with math drills. Some math is best learned by drills, the multiplication tables, for example, so that 7 × 7 brings an automatic response of 49. But poor Corinne. We finally decided that she is allergic—to arithmetic. Then we laugh together and the drills come easier.

Also Melissa's handwriting has left much to be desired. I pointed out her problems until she reminded me, "Mama, a machine makes the writing in the handwriting book." Well, this remained a "problem" to me, if not to my little blonde daughter. Then when a supervisor visited us to check on the girls' work, she took one look at Melissa's handwriting and exclaimed, "What creative handwriting!"

Then I smiled to myself. For Melissa is our artistic daughter, especially enjoying sculpturing and art classes, and I decided that perhaps her handwriting did not have to be machine perfect.

We respect the efforts of devoted teachers, administrators and parents to provide the best education possible for our country's children under the modern system. But we do have many differences of opinion where our children are concerned. We don't condemn those parents who, for whatever reasons, feel the necessity of sending their children out to school. Yet, we have been pleased when other parents, enlightened by our radical experiment, have become more aware of what is happening to their children and, where necessary and possible, have taken some action to change things.

I realize we have had remarkably few problems over the past five years, especially when I listen to other mothers discuss their children's school problems. We have had no insurmountable practical problems, either. We have had only one recurring difficulty, which, though very annoying, is no doubt due to the basic nature of children. We find it is sometimes hard to get the children to willingly accept the school and household responsibilities which we know they can do. We have found that responsibility is a learned ability, not an inherited trait.

We had better admit that children are instinctively selfish, an instinct perhaps related to their survival. They have to learn through patient, repetitive training that unselfishness has its own rewards. Ironically, in our anxiety to teach them these virtues, we find that our own characters are put to the test. So we admit that it is not easy to try to help our children develop good habits and self-discipline, but we feel it is essential to their sound development and future happiness. And we are certain that it is easier on our little family school. We sense that it is the responsible way to love them. In some ways, it would be "easier" to delegate this awesome task to others, but we have chosen to accept the broadest implication of this responsibility.

The rewards of our endeavor have been immense. Our prayers—and we do pray—have been answered. We have not done it by ourselves, nor is the job finished. We are well pleased with our children's scholastic progress thus far, but far more importantly, they are able to think independently and creatively. These are important tools of life. They can think through and express their ideas without excessive concern about what anyone else might think. This desirable independence was a fond hope of ours—independence of the less desirable influence of their peers. At least outwardly, they seem to understand that what others might think is not a good criterion by which to evaluate thoughts or actions.

Recently Corinne gave a three-minute speech for us. The assignment involved choosing a topic, then mentally composing the talk. She stood in our classroom, self-consciously twisting and turning as she began. "I'm going to talk on 'Why My Mother Teaches Me at Home.'"

Listening, I became amazed at her grasp of the reasons we hold home school. She spoke of Christian values and the importance of being with her family.

Melissa listened and even little Bradley stopped his playing, as if he knew something important was in the air. I could feel tears filling my eyes.

When she came to her ending, "I know my mother really loves me so much," I couldn't keep back my tears. Corinne and Melissa's eyes were wet too, and suddenly we looked at each other and burst out in laughter at the absurdity of our tears.

Emotionally they are very stable and basically happy. Much to everyone's apparent surprise, they are not at all dependent on Doug and me in social situations. Dr. Moore commented that they were "very special little hostesses." Although they have encountered some of the grim realities of peer group interaction, they have not been crushed by it. They have—as well as children can be expected—tried to understand and react in line with Christian beliefs and morals. This is difficult to do, but very special to us to see happening. We believe that the security of their home has given them this kind of independence.

Having school at home brings much more than schoolwork. This fall the girls decided that they wanted to sew and I was all for that. We'd work together and I figured they'd begin with aprons or perhaps a simple skirt.

Not my girls. After a talk together they came to me with their choices. They wanted to make Halloween costumes. Melissa chose an angel gown, with rick-rack trim and hook and eye fasteners. Corinne decided that she wanted to be an old-fashioned lady. What does an old-fashioned lady wear but long lace-trimmed sleeves and a long, wide, fully gathered skirt?

They have done virtually all the sewing themselves. Poor Corinne. How many stitches go into hemming the long, *full* skirt of an old-fashioned lady? She worked. We encouraged. She bent over the hemming again . . . and do you know, she finished it in time for Halloween!

Learning, sewing, perseverance . . . education.

Our family life has been enriched by home schooling. The whole family is involved in the learning experience—daddy as well as me. We work together on problems and share responsibilities. We have a calm home despite the fact that the children are here all the time. And the neighborhood children seem to sense their contentment. They come by constantly. Our children are comfortable, not overtired, and not always subjected to the emotionally upsetting experiences of modern schools.

Frequently some of our children's peers will express envy of Corinne's and Melissa's freedom from attending "school." We have sensed, however, some deeper reasons. Although these youngsters may not be able to verbalize their feelings at an early age, they often seem to resent having been sent away from the security and companionship of their homes when they most desired it. Few parents seem to realize this although it is well known by child psychologists. They feel a loss which they can't express or don't get a chance to tell.

We have found that home education is not the total answer to all our child-rearing problems. But it is a rewarding alternative to giving it over to others with less motivation to succeed and less time to give than we have as their parents. The difficulties inherent in raising children, particularly in today's culture, will be with us. At least they are greatly reduced. By keeping our children with us most of the time we have the opportunity to respond to and hopefully remedy the problems as they arise.

Corinne is beginning to ask a lot of questions, thoughtful questions about right and wrong. She shows almost an adolescent concern for certain things. Because of our interaction in home school I can talk with her very easily. She feels free to question. She listens and accepts my guidance. I'm not so naive as to think that this will solve all the problems of the turbulent teen years, but surely open communication between us will make it easier.

One surprise of home school is the degree to which our family life has come to revolve around it. School supplies are big items when I buy for Christmas and birthdays and the best part is that the children are delighted.

One of the biggest events of our year is the day when the school material arrives. Melissa and Corinne helped order their books and supplies and that really makes it special. We're careful to include something for Brad also, so he won't feel left out.

Gradually our basement classroom has assumed the appearance of a "regular" schoolroom, which, of course, it is. Our long bookcase is full to overflowing; a bulletin board, maps and phonics cards cover the wall, while various other teaching aids have their appropriate place. (Bradley, playing with his trucks and cars, keeps our environment from becoming too much like an institution.)

We expect to continue our home education as long as we all benefit. We have discovered that our children are fun to have around once they reach "school age" and we expect to continue to enjoy them a few more years. If the teen years turn out to be more difficult, it may be that they'll need their family even more—even as they resist it in their need to grow up and be independent. This is a goal we all share. The difficulty, if it comes, will be in agreeing on how best to achieve our goal. So far it looks very good. The other youngsters in the neighborhood love and emulate them. So this is an even greater challenge to be good examples.

Certainly we hope as parents, whatever choices our children may make in later years, to stand before our Creator, Who shared His act of creation with us, and to know that we did our best to fulfill the obligations and responsibility He placed on us. He gave us a very special gift when He blessed us with our children.

FOUR

The Builder and the Homemaker
———————————with Pat Graybill———————————

Telling our story is fun for me. We are the Graybills four: Pat, Buck, Bucky, who at this writing is thirteen, and Brent, nine. My husband and I are both high-school graduates. I had most of a year of college in Madison, Tennessee. Buck is a successful building contractor and businessman. I am a homemaker, mother, and self-taught nutritionist. We, like many parents of pre-school children, expected our children to go to school at the usual age of five or six and of course, like most parents, thought our children to be brighter than average and would benefit from early schooling.

"I'm going to take my books and lamb and go to school," our oldest boy, Bucky, announced one day. I remember him standing there on his bed at the age of four. He had a pet lamb and didn't want to leave him out of anything.

On another occasion when we had made a trip to the library, I overheard him saying to himself as he surveyed all the books in the aisle where he stood, "I can't wait until I can read. I'm going to read, read, read." At that time we thought, how cute! He's going to be a scholar by the time he's seven. And we even wondered if it might be damaging to hold him back. But by the time he actually reached between five and six, our ideas about what we wanted for our children were beginning to change. We

44

had been studying the book *Child Guidance* by E. G. White, who
describes how important it is for parents to be the only teacher
until a child reaches eight to ten years of age and the crucial
importance of young children to be much in the out-of-doors
drinking in the fresh air and sunshine. And there were others,
like Angelo Rossi and John Dewey, who also urged later starting
to school.

We had come to the place in our minds that we wanted to
keep Bucky out of school and yet we couldn't make a decision.
We swayed back and forth, for we knew no one who was doing
this. When we would talk to people about it, they would try to
discourage us, suggesting that anyone in his right mind could see
that Bucky is ready for school. Our well-meaning friends and
neighbors thought we were out of our minds, and even we began
to wonder ourselves.

I remember how my husband and I looked across the table at
each other and said, "Why are we thinking like this?" Instinctively we were certain of our course. Yet it ran completely against
"the system."

We really questioned the soundness of our own reasoning.
Worse than that, questions seemed to bubble up all around us.

"What grade are you in?" they would ask Bucky.

"But, I'm not in any school," he would answer with childish
frankness.

"Oh, I bet you're anxious to start."

"No, not especially," he would reply.

"How old are you?" was usually the next question, thinking
that maybe he was big for his age. And when they found he was
eight or nine they would look to us for an explanation of why this
big boy wasn't in school.

This all served to make us keenly aware that we were marching
to the sound of different drums. And to be truthful at that time
we weren't so sure we wanted to be different. After all, it's not
that easy paddling a little two-man canoe against the winds on a
big ocean, and it seemed to us that this was exactly what we were
doing. It was not safe to assume the whole world could be wrong

and we were the only ones right. Those were difficult days for us. But we fully believed that our children were sacred trusts—that God had a plan for our little family—and we prayed that He would give us help in this important decision.

Help came when we needed it most. In August, 1973, the magazine *These Times* came out with an article entitled: "The Dangers of Early Schooling," written by Dr. Raymond S. Moore and Dennis R. Moore. Something like it had been in the *Reader's Digest* the year before. It was as if a window had been opened and we were basking in the warm, beautiful light. The Hewitt Research Center had given practical emphasis and meaning to what we had already been studying. A particular paragraph from that article gave stability and courage to our decision:

> A wealth of research has established that one of a child's primary needs in these formative years is for an environment free of tasks that will tax his brain, and an equally important need is for a setting that provides warmth, continuity, and security. That normal school experience does not successfully meet these needs has been established by three different kinds of studies: those that compare early and later school entrants; those that explore important but little understood changes in the young child's brain; and those that compare the effectiveness of parents and teachers in the development of young children. All three lines of investigation point to a common conclusion: early school, far from being the garden of delights its advocates claim, may actually be a damaging experience.

We sent for still other material available from Hewitt and it was as though our little two-man canoe had just been taken in tow by a big, beautiful ship. Hewitt indeed was throwing us a rope and waving a friendly flag that said, "Come and get on board; we're going the same direction as you." After thinking we were out there on the ocean alone, you can be sure that Hewitt was a very welcome discovery.

Well, we sailed into our first little home school year with no problem. It was quite informal, for Bucky was not yet seven. I spent time with both our boys—reading stories, teaching Bible lessons, how to be helpful in the kitchen and around the house. We spent time out-of-doors studying nature and just being out together. Their daddy often took Bucky, our oldest, with him to work, teaching and talking to him about various aspects of the building business. This on-the-job experience has proven a valuable one, far better than any he could have gotten at school.

When he was seven it was his responsibility to keep the scrap lumber picked up around the job, and he helped with the cleaning when we finished a project. He has learned the wonderful feeling of accomplishment that comes from a job well done. We think this is the highest kind of education.

Our second home-school year was a bit more eventful. By this time our children were three and a half and seven and a half. And of course, by keeping our seven-year-old home, we were breaking Colorado's compulsory school attendance law. We were not sure exactly what to do about this, so we decided to just be quiet and do nothing. But it wasn't very long into the school year before our little boat was again on troubled waters.

It all began on a beautiful fall morning. The boys and I had decided to get out for our morning walk. All of the chores were done—which consisted of making beds, feeding the boys' calf, dog, and kittens—and we had a batch of bread rising in the kitchen. The boys and I had decided to take Oscar, our friendly black Angus calf, to eat the grass around the mailbox at the end of our long lane. We sauntered along, drinking in the morning, just enjoying being together—mother and sons, with our beautiful Angus bull.

We noticed a car stop at the end of our lane. We didn't recognize it, but our curiosity was aroused when presently a gentleman, looking very businesslike, got out of the car. He just stood there watching us from the end of the lane. We were having a good time and not in any hurry. By this time Brent was enjoying the view from Oscar's back.

When we finally reached the end of the lane I asked the man if there was something I could do for him. He introduced himself as the assistant superintendent of schools, and said it had come to his attention that we had a school-age boy who was not in school. I tried to be very calm and confident as I told him he *was* in school, he just wasn't in a formal school.

He was very nice as we discussed our home school program, the differences of our convictions on education and the law. Somehow I felt he was a little impressed with curriculum that morning—"Family Togetherness and Love for Animals."

"I'm just doing my job, Mrs. Graybill," he said.

"Just what do you mean?" I asked.

"We expect you to put your boy in school," he replied.

I remember now that I didn't quite catch the emphasis of his words. I answered him by saying, "Well, we'll just have to cross that bridge when we get to it."

It was about a week later that we came face to face with the realization that we were in fact at that bridge. The school truant officer paid us a friendly visit, and advised us of our rights.

"They do not include teaching your own children past the age of seven," he said, and then added, "Here are some papers that will give you the date that this matter will come to court."

We were startled and somehow unprepared for all of this, but again put the matter in God's hands. We felt in view of how He had led us in the past, He would part the waters again and be our Bridge to the other side. We were impressed to call and talk to Dr. Claude Stansberry, who was the superintendent of schools in Loveland.

"I am sorry," he told us, "But it is my job to uphold the law. There is nothing I can do about it."

"Is there someone at the state level with whom we can talk?" we asked him.

"Why yes," he answered thoughtfully, "I will be glad to make an appointment for you to see Robert M. Hall, the state consultant for accreditation."

So we went to Denver and met with Robert Hall and the state legal counsel, Jane Kardokus. They were very interested in what we were doing and the books we referred them to. They explored alternatives that Section (J) of Statute 123-20-5 provides. They decided to allow us to continue our home school under the supervision of a certified teacher.

Well, God had truly parted the waters again for us. Our answer had come before we had gone to Denver. One evening our good friends Pastor and Mrs. L. A. Vixie visited our home, after they learned of our plight.

"I'm a retired teacher," Mrs. Vixie offered. "If there's anything I can do to help, I'll be glad to fit in."

We agreed to cooperate with a teacher, although I would be doing the actual teaching and it would not involve more than an hour and a half to two hours a day of desk work. After our meeting with the legal counsel, Mr. Hall asked us in to his private office.

"What you are doing," he quietly told us, "is ideal."

We were warmed by his friendly words.

Then he added, "I remember being nailed to a desk as a young student. And I'm sure that this early schooling business is a substantial cause of the high rate of high-school dropouts."

Our home-school program was very relaxed the rest of the year. We did very little book work, for our oldest was just turning eight, and we also knew that boys mature later than girls, although we did do some phonics just for fun.

Since we were living on ten acres of land, the boys could always find plenty to do out-of-doors. When the kids down the road were riding motorcycles, our boys were riding good old Oscar. (My husband told the boys if they could ride Oscar he would let them get horses. We were not in favor of motorbikes.)

What a show I got from my kitchen window almost every afternoon! I'd laugh so hard I'd almost cry. Sometimes Oscar would get bored with it all and go back to eating. So the boy who wasn't riding on top would crank the tail and away they would go again.

Lots of times when the boys were riding their bull, the one at the tail would hang on for dear life and both boys would get a ride at the same time—one on top and the other bobbing along behind. Oscar loved the boys as much as they loved him, and he was so docile I never worried about them. Those were wonderful days and still make my heart sing to remember them.

At the end of the school year when Bucky was eight years and three months, Mrs. Vixie tested him. At first we looked at the wrong test chart, and it appeared that he had not done very well.

"Now, remember, honey," Mrs. Vixie looked at me intently, "you didn't want to sit at the desk with him."

I was crushed, for so much hung on his scores, not only for his case but for others. I couldn't understand it, and tears began to fill my eyes.

"I couldn't have done otherwise," I told her, "if what I've read is right. I wanted my boys free as lambs 'til at least eight."

At that moment she said, "Oh, I'm so sorry, honey. I have read from the wrong chart!"

Then she read the correct scores to me. Bucky was well above average in most subjects and not below average in any! We had followed God's leading and He had blessed.

"He has done so well," Mrs. Vixie said. "I see no reason why you shouldn't go for another year."

So we did. We just took one year at a time. We wanted the boys to be together as long as they could—to help one another, learn from each other and be happy together. Soon we completed five years with them together. Bucky started regular school in the sixth grade, and we did one more year alone with Brent. Even then Brent really benefited from his extra year at home. Up to this time we had spent a little more concentrated time with Bucky because of their age difference. Now we gave our undivided attention to Brent, and it showed.

Out of school many times the boys have done bread demonstrations for me in community health classes. Bucky is also able to tile an entire bath by himself including cutting, placing and grouting of the tile.

During our home school years, we lived a mile and a half from a church school and about three miles from the public school.

We did receive a lot of criticism. People seemed to think that we were not being supportive of our church-school program that was so close to our door. And they didn't mind telling us so. This social pressure was merciless.

When Bucky was ten we did talk to the school about enrolling him.

"He will have to make up all the past work," the teacher told us.

"Why?" we asked.

"For the state records," she insisted.

"But," I protested, "I know the state people and they would never insist on that."

"That's our rule!" She was adamant.

"But," I asked as politely as I could muster, "he is above in most subjects and not below in any."

"Nevertheless . . ."

I was nonplussed. This was supposed to be a trained teacher, certificated, state approved, solid gold, and yet was unable to understand the simplest facts of child development and common sense.

This seemed cruel, even if it was conventional. And it certainly was not sound education. It seemed in some way she wanted to punish us for holding him back. I was so glad for men like Mr. Hall and Mr. Stansberry.

We decided to postpone his enrollment in regular school and continue in our home school. And we never had reason to be sorry. A typical day's schedule would start with morning worship at around 8:00, and it would include some singing, a Bible story or maybe a Bible game and memorizing a Bible text. Then we usually followed with reading, writing and phonics. We wanted a Bible-centered program and Mrs. Vixie approved the Mennonite Rod and Staff material from Crockett, Kentucky. She said it was among the best she had seen.

We always took a long morning break, going for walks, doing some yard and garden work and playing together. We also had math and in the third grade we included science. We finished by noon, and two or three days a week the boys went with their father on the job project. This was great education—physical, industrial education with their own dad!

Now both of our boys have started in school. The old teacher is gone and both of their teachers are happy to have them. Mrs. Jones, Bucky's seventh-grade teacher, says he's always so eager to help and is a good influence on the other children. He has no problem with motivation, always completes his work and does a neat job, too. She gives him a group of younger children to teach—helping with their reading and phonics. This is really great education.

"He gets right to the business," she says. "There is no fooling around."

Brent's teacher says of him, "He's a joy to have in my room. He is a good example and leader to other children, is quick to obey, and also is doing well with his studies."

I tell these things not to stick a feather in our hat, for we must not take the credit. As their parents, we have only tried in our imperfect way to do as God did with the boy Jesus. Oh yes, we've had our ups and downs, and there have been those days when I would have liked to have put them in school and forgotten about it all. But as the days have come and gone, my husband and I have realized our children are not the only ones learning and growing, but in fact we were students too, learning in God's school. God knew all along what we needed when He instituted the family relationship in the first garden school and when He put the Christ child in His father's carpenter shop. It is here in this relationship that characters are formed not only for this life but the life to come—even if the parents have only a high-school education!

FIVE

The Hotel Keepers
————————with Dixie Rice————————

"You mean you'd take your child out of public school and teach her . . . in a hotel?"

"What's the matter? Leslie Sue in trouble at school?"

"Why, afternoons I see her riding her horse just as big as you please. It's a shame, a big girl like that, not in school. What's the matter with her parents anyway?"

Heads shook, people whispered, then asked outright, "Why doesn't Leslie Sue go to school?"

It was July 1977. A year before, my husband and I purchased the Wallace Hotel in Wallace, Nebraska. The hotel had been closed and boarded up for ten years, yet we felt secure that with his mechanical and electrical expertise, Les could fix up the old building. An aggressive person, my husband is one who stays with a job once he starts it. We were certain that we'd be able to turn the hotel into a business that would afford us a living.

So we moved from Shelton to Wallace in August 1976, and Leslie Sue transferred to the sixth grade in the public school there. We were not entirely happy with the situation, for her grades had been going downward since the fourth grade and we couldn't pinpoint why. We wondered about the crowded classrooms, and teachers unable to give individual attention, yet we had no other choice.

53

Our son had graduated three years before, and we'd been more and more concerned as we had witnessed the deterioration of moral and educational quality of his school books. It seemed they did little to promote love and respect for America, but rather encouraged the children to believe that they were good in themselves, that man is all-powerful. Of course, being public schools with the separation of church and state, there could be no mention of God or religion.

We were not only unhappy generally with the textbooks and the questions they raised in the students' minds. Specifically we agonized as we saw evolution taught as fact without any balance whatsoever of the biblical point of view. There was never a hint in history of God's leading.

The drug use among students deeply disturbed us and the early, intense relationships between boys and girls. We sought to instill high standards and values in our daughter but the public school situation seemed to slash across almost everything we believed.

And yet, until July 1977, we knew of no alternative but to send our twelve-year-old daughter back to public school.

Then I saw an ad in a magazine for the home study program of the Christian Liberty Academy, the CLA. Interested, I showed it to Les and Leslie Sue. They shared my cautious excitement. I mean, we wondered if such "correspondence work" would prove as valuable as advertised. We prayed about it and finally decided to call the number listed. We were on our way.

They sent us the Iowa Tests of Basic Skills with instructions on how to administer them. These tests were familiar to Leslie Sue as she'd taken them in both the Shelton and Wallace schools. She finished the tests and we sent them in to be evaluated. They showed her to be average in most subjects but only on the fifth grade level in math, and she was entering the seventh.

We paid the Academy's tuition, then $185 a year, and they requested and received her records from Wallace School District. The textbooks arrived and with no inkling of where our decision would lead us, Leslie Sue opened the books and began to study.

Our classroom was our in-the-process-of-being-remodeled apartment on the ground floor of the hotel. Leslie Sue and I arranged desks facing each other in a corner near her room. This wasn't a correspondence school, I suddenly realized. I, her mother, with a high school education, was the teacher of the new Rice Christian Academy! Les and I each had only a semester of college.

We concentrated heavily on math that year, and English and science—her weakest areas. The textbooks delighted us. All subjects were related to the principles of Christian love for God and society found in the Bible.

We found that math is meaningless without God, for He set up the boundaries and absolutes which make math an exact science. History is truly His story as well. We see God in the working of science, from the intricacies of the circulatory system to the incredible migration of the arctic tern.

In short, soon after we saw the textbooks, we had no fears about our new program, no doubts that we were doing the right thing. As her main teacher, the CLA instructed me to proceed with the books and lessons, dividing the pages by the number of weeks of school we planned—thirty-six weeks. I sat at my desk, my daughter across from me and corrected her work at once so she could easily see and learn from her mistakes. It's a process known as "immediate feedback" and is lauded by teachers as the best way to learn. Unfortunately, few teachers in their overcrowded classrooms are able to do it. We now understand better why so many geniuses got their education by tutor.

Leslie Sue progressed rapidly, her work coming along so nicely that we were actually surprised when the trouble started. Living on Main Street in a town of 240 is like living in the proverbial fishbowl. Every ripple you make can be seen from all sides.

Maybe we should have seen it coming, but then it wouldn't have made any difference. We'd had a number of questions from the townspeople and we'd listened to their advice and explained our position. Yet the visit by the local school superintendent took us by surprise.

He didn't seem impressed by our home setup or the fact that Leslie Sue had quietly sprung ahead in most of her subjects. His eyes took in our unfinished "classroom," and our young daughter bent alone over her work.

"You're breaking the law," he told us, "the compulsory attendance law."

"But she's going to school at home," we countered, pointing out her textbooks and workbooks.

The man left. But the first clouds of concern began to shadow our home school. We determined to ignore them, to keep on with the school work.

The county superintendent called next with more questions and an ultimatum. Finally the deputy County Attorney filed charges against us for *child neglect* in the area of education. "Criminal child neglect," they finally called it. One of our local lawmen came into our hotel and placed a subpoena in our hands. We were to appear in juvenile court on October 25. Strange emotions went through our hearts. Here we were actually charged as criminals. It all seemed so wrong.

Of course this was far beyond our scope of experiences so we didn't know what to expect but nothing could have prepared us for what happened. A pretrial, they called it, an arraignment and none of us were asked to testify. But the judge—a woman— proceeded to try to damage us as much as possible.

"We have the authority to take your child out of your home," she told us sternly. This seemed a starkly cruel threat.

"You realize, Leslie Sue, that you don't have to listen to your parents. We can appoint you a lawyer." This message to our daughter!

"You have the right to go to school, Leslie Sue. You have the right to be with other children your own age. Your parents can't take this away from you." Leslie Sue couldn't believe her ears.

We didn't answer; we didn't try to answer. At that point, what could we say?

October 25, our first day in court, was also our daughter's thirteenth birthday.

We were advised to obtain a lawyer for ourselves and a second one for our daughter. She could not use our lawyer because we "might influence him," the court stated and eventually they appointed a man, a public defender, for her.

We left the courtroom numbed by the unreality of what had happened behind those walls. Our courts, our protectors! We felt shafted as the judge actually tried to turn our daughter against us! We found it unbelievable that she threatened to take Leslie Sue from our home, just because we elected to use Christian home-school work rather than the public classroom.

Yet, in a strange way, we were not frightened but strengthened by the judge's threats. She had only succeeded in binding us closer together, to determine to support each other and to see the problem through—and win!

We felt God on our side, so were not unduly concerned.

We contacted Attorneys Tom Guilfoyle and Craig Swoboda in Omaha, who gladly took our case. "Mrs. Rice, are you willing to go to jail for your beliefs?" Attorney Guilfoyle asked me.

For an instant I was taken aback, then told him, "Yes, I am willing to go to jail."

What had I said? What would my husband and daughter think? I posed the question to them and told them my reply. We discussed the possible results of our decision to keep Leslie Sue learning at home and concluded that we were not quitters. God would see us through. That discussion marked a turning point in our attitude toward our prosecution. From that time on we never had a fear or even a period of doubt.

After the public defender talked to Leslie Sue, he realized the seriousness of her beliefs and her love for her family. Nevertheless, the deputy county attorney—another woman—determined to press charges. We were told that she had a small child kept daily by a baby sitter, never fondling the child or caring for it herself.

On the day we appeared in county court, friends and well-wishers staged a rally for us on the courtsteps before the trial began. We, like others, found that most people and most of the media are still for parents' rights.

The trial lasted two days. Our attorney maintained that the

law was vague and virtually impossible to enforce. He laid the foundations of our belief in God before the court and asserted that by *not* teaching our child Christian principles and precepts, we would be disobeying God.

Pastor Lindstrom of the Christian Liberty Academy came a long distance to testify in our behalf. The judge listened, his face impassive.

The court belabored the fact that I was not a certified or qualified teacher. Again and again they returned to the tired refrain that we were denying Leslie Sue social contact with her peers. "She'll never be able to take her proper place in society without this contact," they said. "It's the state's duty to see that all children are properly prepared to take their place in society." As drug addicts? we questioned silently. With the unfortunate ones that drop out? As unwed mothers and fathers? As high school graduates who never learned to read, the too-often product of a lifetime of education in public schools?

At the end of two long days the judge found us guilty as charged and ordered us to pay court costs.

We'd gone to court with the threat of Leslie Sue's removal still heavy over our home and were prepared to whisk out of the county—or state—if necessary. However, the judge conceded that since she'd stayed at home these months with no apparent ill effects, she might as well remain a while longer.

We'd lost the battle but were confident that with God's help we'd win the war.

We immediately appealed the decision to district court and they scheduled our court appearance for July, 1978. By then the local papers had discovered the story and came to talk with us. They treated us fairly and this led to many opportunities to visit with television reporters and personnel. So not all our surprises were unpleasant. We found the media quite open to our views. We saw them several times, went by the studio to leave them answers—material on home study and also on our problems with the public school system.

Because of this publicity an interested person sent us an article by a man we'd never heard of, a Dr. Raymond Moore. He is a developmental psychologist with a specialty in early childhood. It seemed he had done a lot of research in early-childhood education and home schools. We forwarded the article to Leslie's lawyer and he eventually contacted Dr. Moore. Judge Lindsay Arthur of the St. Paul, Minnesota juvenile court had also recommended Dr. Moore to Attorneys Guilfoyle and Swoboda.

Dr. Moore asked that Leslie Sue be tested by an unbiased party, suggesting that we go to our state university which he thought would be best respected by the judge. So at our own expense we went to Omaha, Nebraska, where a professor at the University of Nebraska, Dr. Valerie Cook, administered the Iowa Basic Skills tests and other measures during our four-day stay. The testing over, we could do little but wait. Spring flowered into summer, the days warmed, then grew hot. June. July.

The professor from the University of Nebraska agreed to come testify for us. Dr. Moore came, too. We met him at his motel before the trial. He asked Leslie Sue a few questions privately and also with us, had her diagram some sentences (and said that most students of her age were unable to do them correctly, though she had no problems) and gave her some other tests. Also, he seemed curious about her attitude toward us and her values as well as her grades. He seemed pleased. So we felt better. We'd been doing our homework for six months. We'd felt God's leading and guidance as we developed our defense. Now we were ready for court.

Dr. Cook first testified for us, bringing a graph she'd made comparing Leslie's scores on the Iowa Tests of Basic Skills. It showed her low scores at the beginning of seventh grade—then after a year of home study—their dramatic rise, especially in math. She had averaged two to three grades' improvement in her studies during that home school year.

Again, the state, in the person of its prosecuting attorney Marianne Vainiunas, built its criminal case against us. She tried to embarrass Dr. Moore, our leading witness, by asking him if he was a born-again Christian. If he had said "yes," as most Christians would have expected, she would have cornered him and put him on the defensive. But he was not so easily trapped.

"What," he asked her, "is *your* definition of a born-again Christian?"

She obviously didn't expect this and sort of stammered out what was a really good description.

"If that is your definition," Dr. Moore replied, smiling, "I am one."

She dropped the subject like a hot potato and got into our case by trying to develop the premise that our daughter would be socially disturbed because of the lack of what she called "proper social contact with a peer group." But her idea of what was proper was not the same as ours.

Dr. Moore proved to be a godsend against this argument. He testified with evidence based on his experience as a psychologist and public educator and on his well-known research that children progress much faster socially, emotionally, academically and with greater stability in a warm and consistent home atmosphere where they best develop a sense of self-worth, especially during their early years.

He presented as examples two cases where the kids were kept out until their teen years and how they did all the work required to keep up with their peer group in only one year. He enumerated the benefits of home school. In fact, from his research and experience, he easily shot down every argument the state had against us.

We thanked God for Leslie's progress and Dr. Moore's testimony and felt certain we'd win our case. "Give God all the glory," Dr. Moore said. "He was testing you." And sure enough, Judge Keith Windrum of the district court did rule in our favor even though he was well known for his loyalties to the public schools. We thanked God for a fair judge.

Prosecutor Vainiunas nevertheless appealed Judge Windrum's decision to the Supreme Court of Nebraska. We waited again in prayer. Then, the Supreme Court ruled unanimously in our favor. So with Nebraska's official approval, we entered our second year of home school. We thanked God again for fair judges.

Leslie Sue follows a fairly strict schedule from 8:45 to 2:30, and is doing outstanding work in her studies. I taught her an hour and a half or so a day at the start. But she is now fifteen and a high-school junior in our family school and I hardly teach her at all any more. Remember, four years ago she was floundering in the sixth grade at the local public school. People marvel at the excellence of her education. Even her friends acknowledge it, some wishing they could do the same. But she also helps me in the hotel three or four hours a day making beds, cooking, cleaning and being a first-rate assistant manager. We think this balance of work and study is a great advantage to her. It has made her prompt, industrious, responsible, dependable and courteous to all.

Yet the isolation of private study has not kept her from making friends. She has more than ever, and friends who are really worthy friends. She also has kept her interest in her horses, in taking proper care of them, in riding and in raising a colt.

One subject she's taken from CLA that she's especially enjoyed is a Christian charm course. It teaches the girls how to sit, stand and walk properly. It outlines foods necessary for a good complexion. But running like a thread through all that is the admonition that no matter how pretty you are on the outside, you need a new heart to be a beautiful person. This is the kind of education we were praying for.

Many people come to us, some worried about taxes or having to pay court costs, and asking our advice in making their decision to begin a home school. We tell them that it's not a question of money anymore. It's a question of survival for our children.

SIX

The Army Wife and the Intelligence Officer

—————————with Betty Gerbozy—————————

Meet Seth. A typical little boy; a happy little boy. Small for his age and cautious by nature. Blond, blue-eyed . . . those blue, blue eyes magnified by the thick lens of his glasses. Seth, my son, they told me, was quite possibly going blind.

Where else to start but at the beginning?

My husband's intelligence work sent him over the world and soon after we married we moved to Japan. I'd never much wanted to go to Japan. Living in Europe was my dream, but I fell in love with our small island—and its warm, friendly people—a mere 500 miles from Siberia. Such was the U.S. Army.

The weather stayed cold and raw most of the time. The children seemed to get one eye-ear-nose-and-throat infection after the other. Seth had his share, too, but nothing hit so badly as the illness that struck at sixteen months of age when we moved back to the States: diarrhea, very probably caused by the emotional upset of moving. The illness can be devastating to small children, as it upsets the salts and electrolytes in their system and dehydrates them.

My sensitive little man. We poured fluids into him to offset the loss. We took him to doctors along the trip. We medicated him. Nothing helped. I walked him, sang to him, whispering the songs in his ear. It became my joy, whispering songs to him as I danced him about in our new home. Gradually he improved, began to gain back the weight lost by illness.

An intense ear infection invaded when he was three, in both ears. He had inflammation, earaches and a slow recovery. Later, when he was eight, we would wonder if that caused permanent damage. It's so hard to know.

Seth was three and a half when we went to Europe, my dream location. Our second child would be born soon.

The beauty of Europe, the blending of the old with the new, the snow-powdered mountaintops—none of this could make up for the hostility of our neighbors toward Americans, especially toward the military, and our work was partly of this nature.

Deborah was born, fitting neatly into our snug apartment, into our lives.

At age four, we discovered that Seth suffered from extreme astigmatism. This was so severe that the ophthalmologist expressed great surprise that his eyes were not crossed. The doctor could not tell us if his eyes would ever improve, or if they would deteriorate as the years passed, and he insisted that an opthalmologist should examine him every six months to make sure they were not getting worse.

Glasses were prescribed with heavy, thick lenses because his eyes were so terribly bad. At first the doctor planned to give Seth glasses in two stages, starting with less-strong lenses at first so that he could become accustomed to the change in vision before prescribing the really strong ones. We were warned that he might fight them, that we could expect problems, but there were none.

I can still see him the first time he put them on; such a slight little fellow for such heavy glasses. We waited, but there were no problems. He just seemed so relieved to be able to focus on the world—to be able to *see*—that they didn't bother him.

We began our quest for schooling for Seth when he turned five years old. Looking ahead, we wondered where we'd send him. The organization my husband worked for provided a school, but as a previous teacher myself, I was not assured of their compe-

tence and concern for children. Not all, of course. Some teachers were excellent, but most seemed poorly trained, and more
interested in being in Europe than in teaching their students.

We began to think of teaching our children at home.

Because we are Christians, we preferred a Christ-centered curriculum. Because of Seth's unique problems, and because someone whose judgment we valued had observed that children do
well to be kept out of school until they are more emotionally and
physically mature—we planned to wait until he was eight to
begin.

In 1970 we attended a workshop that included talks by a man
from the states who was prominent in religious education. We
met with him, thinking he could give us guidance in planning a
home-study program. When we mentioned that we planned to
delay study until Seth turned eight, the man became scornful.

"Children mature faster than they used to," he declared.
"They know so much more nowadays because of television," he
said. "A six-year-old should be in school."

We left the interview feeling strangely chastened and disappointed, though unshaken in our belief that early schooling
would not be good for Seth.

The seasons blurred one into the other, spring dripping into
summer, summer fading before the blaze of autumn, and winter
lingering long after we longed for spring. In due time, when Seth
was six and a half, we went back to the States.

This time we stayed twelve months.

During this time, with Seth going on seven, I felt pressured to
enroll him in some form of school. I wanted to spare him the
negative remarks of neighbors or children and legal problems
that could arise.

So we ordered kindergarten lessons from a study-at-home correspondence school.

It was a useless venture, a waste of my time. And even worse,
totally unnecessary. The work was so simple that there was no
challenge. It was nothing more than busy work.

It was during this time that he developed hearing problems.

Then we received instructions to move again. Back to Europe.

Before we left, we had Seth evaluated at a Rehabilitation Center, specifically for the purpose of having his ears checked. In the process his eyes were checked also.

The staff was kind, considerate and gave him a number of different tests. At the end of the day, the evaluation was completed, and we were told that Seth had a severe learning problem. His eyes, not his ears, were the cause.

The diagnosis: extreme astigmatism, no depth perception, both eyes working independently of each other. Furthermore, he probably saw split images or double images of everything, not to mention that the words on a page didn't remain stationary, but wandered around as he tried to focus on them.

These are the eyes of the child I was trying to push through kindergarten, I thought.

They also tested him for maturity in several areas and his maturity checked out at six years even though he would be eight in a few months.

We saw a psychologist at the end of the evaluation, and were told bluntly that if we'd put Seth in school at the usual school age, he would have been ruined—devastated—by now. The man added as gently as he could that Seth would probably never read well, if indeed he would ever read at all. However, he instructed us in some eye exercises for Seth and gave us some first-grade books. We were to begin tutoring Seth by teaching him letters of the alphabet. The psychologist told me to open the book to page one and say the letters of each word one time. Seth then must tell me the letters, and I must let him flounder around, guessing as many as five times before I would give him the correct answer again. What I did any loving parent can do.

After he had "learned" the alphabet in this way (and also learned to hate learning, I thought) I was to continue the procedure with words.

This teaching method, we were told, had two purposes. The first, to teach him to read. The second, to break his independent spirit and make him more docile.

The psychologist viewed Seth's so-called lack of hearing as inattention and a form of rebellion. Seth will cry in frustration, he told me, but I must ignore this and continue with the program. Starting at five minutes a day, I should soon lengthen the time to fifteen minutes or more. I should keep in touch with the psychologist by writing once a week.

We left the Rehabilitation Center, books in our arms and Seth by the hand, our minds a tangle of questions. Was this good advice? Where was the motivation for him to learn the alphabet? Where and how would he find joy in learning? Is this any way to treat a child?

Many weeks later we were settled in our new home, part of a longer, close complex of families—about 150 children around us. At last I began the teaching program prescribed by the Center.

As predicted, Seth resisted. I didn't have his attention. I couldn't keep his attention. Forcing him to guess letters that had no meaning to him was a nightmare and after two or three sessions it struck me as little less than brainwashing.

Besides, *I didn't want to break his will.* I viewed his will and his individuality as sacred before God. I wanted to guide Seth. I wanted to develop his personality, to make reading—if possible—a thing to be enjoyed. I didn't want to fight him, to force him, my son. He was normally obedient. Yet, after two or three stormy, tearful sessions, we abandoned the "program."

It was then that I set up our dining room as a classroom. I was able to get an eight-foot blackboard which I placed against one wall and taped the alphabet in large letters above it; also numerals 0 to 9. I put large—8½ × 11—phonics cards with pictures on a tall breakfront that we used as a room divider.

School was ready to begin.

I started with the short vowel sounds since vowels determine the sound of the word. The first sound we tackled was the short *a*, the "ah" sound.

We began by Seth listening to a group of words as I said them. "*Bat . . . can . . . ran . . .*" Then he looked in a mirror and observed his own mouth saying the words with the short *a*. Next I had him feel my mouth, neck muscles, cheeks, etc., as I said the words. Then he felt the movements of his face as he repeated the words.

I next had him put his head down on the table and listen as I slowly said a group of words. "*Bat . . . can . . . rain.*"

"Now, tell me which of those words have the short *a*, the "ah" sound."

He looked up, his eyes large and serious behind the bottle-glass lens. Oh, how I loved him during those minutes when his face wrinkled with concentration. He hesitated. "Bat?" he questioned, unsure.

"Put your head down again, Seth. Now listen. The short *a*. The 'ah' sound."

The pale yellow head bent obediently to the table.

"Bat. Can. Rain."

He looked up, a smile tiptoeing across his face all the way to his eyes. "Bat and can," he declared.

"That's right, Seth. That's good," I complimented. "Oh, you listened so well."

We did this over and over again.

Seth became restless. His attention span was short. We worked. We took a break. We worked again. We began using pictures, dozens and dozens of pictures that I'd collected. We'd go through ten to fifteen pictures of items whose names illustrated a certain sound. The next day I'd use different pictures illustrating the same sound. We reviewed constantly, not going on to something new until the first was thoroughly learned.

As he learned the sounds, we practiced the letters. First A's. We wrote A's in the air with our fingers. We put the same motions on paper. Crooked A's scattered across the page. Then, they stood taller, straighter . . . now proud soldiers marching in formation.

At first Seth's progress was more like one step forward and five backwards. One day he couldn't do anything right; I couldn't keep his attention, he was restless and uninterested. The next day he'd do beautifully, only to follow that by several days of seemingly total amnesia and frustration.

If I were doing it over again, I would not have started teaching him until he was nine or ten. After all, he'd been diagnosed as having only six-year maturity. But I felt like I raced against time. The doctors had told us he might go blind. The psychologists said he might never learn to read. I felt an urgency to lead him (not push him), to keep his interest up, to teach him to read.

Often, so often our "school" ended in frustration for us both. Often I stopped early because he had reached his limit of endurance. Our classtime was rarely more than two or two and a half hours. This included math and handwriting. The rest of the time he could run and play or help me around the house.

I taught in other ways, however, as he learned to do chores about the apartment. He vacuumed and dusted. He washed potatoes for us to bake. He and Deborah washed and tore lettuce for salad. When we ate, I'd point out that a protein entrée and green and yellow vegetables gave them vitamins they needed.

During these early months he still had trouble hearing. Reaching back in my mind to his babyhood, I recalled the hours spent whispering little songs into his ears. Again, when he seemed unable to hear me, I'd put my mouth to his ear and whisper . . . whisper softly. He would hear and understand.

There were problems with neighbors during these two years of home teaching overseas. I always kept him in the house until noon so that his school absence was not so apparent. We lived close to many schools. Our lives and habits were open to them.

The word "retarded," was whispered around about Seth, then spoken aloud. It seemed vile, obscene—the way people said it.

It became necessary for me to stay outside with the children, so they wouldn't be hurt by the continual taunting and snide remarks. I planned that time into my daily schedule. Parents came to me, offering advice, some demanding that I send Seth— big boy that he is—to school.

Our situation was unique, living in a foreign country, yet we were pretty much left alone by officials to tutor Seth as we chose. We were working for Americans, so they could not go to the country's courts to prosecute us, a blessing that I realized and was thankful for.

And so we continued. One step forward . . . five backwards, it seemed at times, but times changed. We finished the vowel sounds and began consonants. Math became part of our routine. I had an abacus, a "bead-chart," I called it, and we began with the basics—one plus one equals two.

The beauty of a one-to-one relationship is that it lets you know just where your child is at any given time. You can work immediately to encourage or correct.

And slowly, oh so slowly at first, then faster and faster, Seth learned to read. We kept on with the phonics. My review became more complicated and I constantly devised new ways to keep it interesting. In about two years—when he was ten or eleven—Seth had become an excellent reader.

He read the newspaper sent from the States and the *Reader's Digest*. He had good comprehension of what he read and his oral reading became better than many children's.

Seth. Age twelve. Those frantic, fearful early days behind us. He could hold his own in a classroom, I thought, and felt proud of the hours upon hours he'd spent studying in our little home school.

Then we were transferred back to the States.

Because he'd had no formal schooling, we hesitated to place him in a grade he wouldn't be prepared for. So we tentatively enrolled him in the fourth grade, asking that he be tested and placed in a higher grade as soon as possible—if the testing proved him to be really capable.

Early in the school year Seth took the Iowa Basic Skills test, and scored in the 99th percentile in nearly every subject. In reading he scored in the 98th percentile; in math slightly lower. Yet, they never tested him for grade placement. The professor in charge of testing at the school simply washed his hands of Seth and the whole affair.

Seth coasted—with no encouragement or challenge from his teacher—all year long.

The next year, fifth grade, the situation changed. The teacher worked with her students, she led them, she guided them to do more than they thought they were able. A good year, the fifth grade. We were encouraged.

Grade six. Seth, age fourteen. Again, unfortunately, the teacher did little but assign busywork. He coasted, doing no more than required. Good teacher, poor teacher, this is school.

Sometimes I worried because he was so much older than the others in his grade. He remained small for his age—he fit in that way—but I shuddered to think what it would be like if he were six foot and built like a football player. Would they still demand that he finish *every bit of every grade,* even though all evidence points that he could go on to more advanced studies? Where is the challenge, the incentive to excel when everything is too easy for the students?

We kept Deborah out of school until she was eight. We then enrolled her in the first grade, where she did better than good. She learned quickly—immediately grasped concepts that the six-year-olds had difficulty with, which is only normal—and was double promoted between the second and fourth grade.

Yet, she could not enter the fourth grade with students her age *until she completed all the third grade book work and workbooks.* To do this extra she had to stay after school two days a week and work on third grade work during school hours. If she knew the studies well, why all the repetition?

Do I sound unhappy with our school system? I am. By far the overseas teachers in our experience have been—I hate to say it— lazy in actuality. Is merely following the outlines in the Teacher's Guide of every textbook, *teaching?* Is assigning endless pages of workbooks really teaching? Shouldn't teaching invoke an excitement for learning, a challenge for even the small child to reach beyond his known grasp and achieve more than he knew that he could? Are children manacled to every workbook page?

Must not the physical and emotional side of the child be

considered as well as the mental? Learning *must* be more than filing information in the appropriate slots in the brain.

And yet, after a few years in classes, our children's idea of school is still to fill out endless and mindless workbook pages. The older children already recognize for themselves that workbooks rarely do more than keep the pupils busy. Their major complaint has been the hours they spent in school for no purpose.

Often the teacher took away the recess and noon-hour playtime as punishment for sundry offenses. In one classroom the teacher shortened the time allowed to eat lunch as punishment, so that often they hardly had time to gulp it down. And this only outraged the students. They didn't learn or change their behavior from experiencing the punishment, especially when the entire classroom received this punishment for the misdeeds of a few in the teacher's vain hope that the guilty ones would confess and release the others from confinement. I could go on. But the sum of it all is that I am thankful for the privilege of home school.

It seems long ago and far away—and yet in some ways only the day before yesterday—that a slight blond boy bent over phonics picture cards in our dining room classroom. He's not so little any more; he's beginning to grow taller.

No longer frustrated and angered by words that scampered across the page as he tried to focus on them, he's an excellent reader and a good student.

We've moved—again. The last move, we hope, for a long time. The kids are in a small school that has a work-study program. * They're challenged. They're excited. They're happy.

And that's another whole story.

---

* Betty Gerbozy now directs the Child Development Center at Weimar College, Box A, Weimar, CA 95736, where she has developed "a home-school curriculum tailored to your child's needs, which strongly supports delayed formal schooling until at least age eight, but provides informal helps for younger children."

SEVEN

The Teacher and the Carpenter
─────────────with Ruth Nobel─────────────

It wasn't that our kids weren't happy in school. There hadn't been any big problems. But my husband and I still somehow were not satisfied with their education . . .

Perhaps I should introduce us all before I go further. I'm Ruth, your everyday, average housewife and mother of—count them—seven. I taught school for four years before settling down to raise my own little red schoolhouse.

My husband is Peter, a former schoolteacher who is presently a carpenter. We are fortunate in that we live on seventy-seven acres in Michigan, including pasture, woods, sand dune and swamp.

The kids from the top down are Abigail (thirteen), Naomi (twelve), Priscilla (ten), Eve (nine), Charity (seven), Luke (five), and Hope (two) is our little caboose. They're average kids whose interests range from crocheting (Abigail's working on two bedspreads in her spare time) to cornet (Naomi's joy) to horses and bike riding.

As I said, they were normal kids, and contented at school. But we weren't entirely satisfied.

We'd already chosen a Christian school over the public ones because our basic beliefs and philosophy differed drastically from that taught in public school. We believe, for example, in the

Biblical account of Creation whereas evolution is taught as fact in public schools with little or no teaching of creationism allowed.

Peter and I have taught our family that God and the Bible are final authority in all matters. The public schools regard man and science as final authority.

And then the standards of both teachers and students in the public schools are different from those we want for our kids. We felt it was counter-productive to expose our kids to smoking and swearing, pot peddling and early dating when we didn't want all *that* for them.

In short, the basic philosophy of the public school seemed materialistic—to make money, get *things*, enjoy life.

Our philosophy includes the belief that all learning should enable us to become better acquainted with God and serve Him better. Therefore we chose a Christian school.

Two years ago, however, we began to have problems, even with their program. There were doctrinal differences from our viewpoint and we found the discipline lax in the junior high. We wanted a change for our children, but didn't quite know where to go.

Then by chance—of course, we know it wasn't really by chance—my brother-in-law saw an ad in a magazine.* The ad offered a home-study program for children, using textbooks based on the Bible and the philosophy that God is, that He loves and guides, and is sovereign over every part of our lives.

We investigated it further. We liked what we found. We wanted to try it.

I guess you've got to be a little bit crazy to even think of teaching five children at home, what with a house and garden to care for too. Unless, you believe that God wants more for your kids than their school can give them, and that He is leading you down a new road.

---

*Home Study Program of the Christian Liberty Academy, 203 East Camp McDonald Road, Prospect Heights, IL 60070.

We believed that and we started the adventure.

Our girls were in grades six, five, four, two and kindergarten. They weren't altogether excited about the change.

May I be candid? Neither was I. Oh, Peter didn't see any problems. Me, *I* saw myriads of them!

Then there were fears—the law, and lack of friends for them to play with, not to mention negative reactions from family and friends. Could I handle teaching plus housework, meals, mountains of laundry, and two pre-schoolers?

Could I do all this and stay physically able?

And sane?

Good question. I'm not, and never was, Supermom. But I wanted to give it a try.

I believe that a healthy approach is to prepare as much as possible ahead of time, begin school, then meet each problem as it occurs.

So . . . ahead of time we set up each study area individually. I knew that with two little ones I would not be able to supervise them constantly and felt that separating the kids this way would minimize the temptation to waste time by waiting and "goofing around." Whatever the work area you decide upon, it should be supplied when you're ready to start.

It's also a good idea to familiarize yourself with each child's textbooks to know where you're heading and how long it should take you to get there.

We stay on a 180-day school schedule, and stick closely to it. Because we are generally where we should be in the textbooks, we feel free to take a day off now and then for other important activities, "field trips," and such.

Back now, to the beginning and the girls. I think that their changing from their regular school to our home school was something like I experienced many times over as a child. A minister's daughter, we moved several times during my school years and after each move there was about a two-month adjustment. During that time I "dragged my feet" against anything the new school had to offer, and looked back longingly through rose-tinted glasses at my former situation.

Our girls weren't rebellious about our decision to teach them at home. We've raised them to respect our guidance, but there was a definite period of adjustment. One suggestion I would have for parents planning a "home school," is that you try to anticipate what your child will miss from his "regular" school. Since art is something our kids looked forward to, we included a Friday art class from the start.

Recognizing their need for friends, we changed our visiting habits. Instead of getting a babysitter for them and *our* visiting friends from 8:00–12:00 on Friday nights, now we have a family over for supper from 6:00–10:00. The children have a great time while we adults talk. They also play with neighbor children and cousins.

I hope this doesn't sound like a sacrifice—this rearranging of our social lives—because it isn't. It's something Peter and I have chosen to do and we enjoy it.

After your school begins, you'll no doubt run into unique and unanticipated problems. We did. To begin, we discovered that we didn't have a globe, so we bought one for Christmas.

Our recreation (and this is of utmost importance, the physical side of education) needed help. We were able to get a secondhand volleyball and net, basketball and rim, etc. Birthday gifts have included a ping pong set and sliding saucers for winter recess.

My teaching methods evolved as the needs arose, and I'm sure that you—like me—will develop your own shortcuts to streamline your program.

For example, I made correcting and planning a one-step process. As I correct Eve's math, I see they're all correct, so I check (√) only every other row on the next three pages for the following day's assignment. I think: why write out lesson plans, or spend a lot of time the next day assigning lessons? By that time, I may have forgotten yesterday's performance.

The Academy supplies us with books, primarily from Beka Books and Rod and Staff Publishers at a cost of about one fifth the costs of the tuition and expenses in a church or private school, not to mention other costs of transportation, incidentals, etc. And we are delighted with the Christian emphasis present in these books.

We send in finished work about every four weeks. They send in report cards four times a year and periodic update sheets. They encourage us to call or write with any questions that come up.

The Iowa Basic and Stanford Achievement tests are sent each fall. We give them to the children and send them in for correction. All in all, we've been very happy working with the Academy to educate our children. The learning material is mostly self-teaching except for kindergarten and the first grade.

They give legal advice—but do not provide a lawyer—and that brings us to another part of the story.

Two months after beginning, we received visits from the truant officer and were subsequently charged with truancy.

A district court hearing was held on our case and both sides were given thirty days to file briefs. We were representing ourselves at first, but then two attorneys—John W. Whitehead of Washington, D.C., who became our head lawyer, and Stuart D. Hubbell of Traverse City, our local counsel—became interested in our case. They saw it as one concerning religious freedom and the separation of church and state. They represented us in court without fee. The expenses involved such as plane fares were paid by the Catholic League. We are not Roman Catholics; however, Mr. Hubbell is. Robert Anderson, Esq., from the Catholic League in Milwaukee, also attended our trial. We found that the basic trial is very important, especially if there is a possibility that the case may be appealed. We were babes in the woods, so to speak. Their help was special. We did not dispute the fact that we were not sending our children to either a public or private school outside our home. However, we maintained that we were not guilty of the truancy charge because we were educating our children in a "satellite school" of the Christian Liberty Academy.

We chose this method of educating our youngsters because of our religious beliefs.

Publicity for our cause began to grow, then snowball. Mr. Jack

Waters,* head of a Christian Schools Organization in Michigan, included our letter of information on his mailing list of pastors and schools. Some of these, in turn, put it on their mailing lists, and we found that in this manner, quite a large region became aware of our legal problems. Many people wrote or called us to share their concern and encouragement, and many also attended the trial.

The basic problem was that the State demanded that school children be taught—or supervised—by a certified teacher. I happened to be a teacher, with a degree in elementary education from Calvin College, but am uncertified.

To obtain and maintain certification would not make me a better teacher. It would not cause my children to learn faster. And it would violate our religious conviction that we are responsible to God for the education of our children.

Professor Donald Erickson of the University of San Francisco and formerly of the University of Chicago, testified that there is no evidence that a teaching certificate proved teacher competence. And, he stated, children in private schools consistently do better on standardized tests than do public school students even though many private schools do not require teacher certification.

In the meantime, the children were evaluated by an educational psychologist—given intelligence and psychological tests.

We knew they were okay. Would the tests bear that out?

The evaluation indicated that our five school age kids were above average in intelligence and had an educational level well ahead of other kids their age.

There is not time nor space to include all the details, but needless to say, we felt God's leading and guidance as we defended our position. On December 14, 1979, we read in the Benton Harbor, Michigan, *Herald Palladium*:

"Judge Says Religious Couple Can Teach Children at Home."

---

*Director of Christian Schools Organization, Jack Waters, 7306 East Atherton Road, Davison, MI 48423

Then, "The goal of the Michigan statute is not to have certified teachers but to educate students. . . . Certification is the State's way of having a set standard for the education of children. If certification conflicts with religious beliefs, then the State has to find another way to deal with that."

We were just thankful to have the trial behind us and to start anew on our study.

A typical day's schedule is:

6:30—I fix breakfast and Peter's lunch.

7:00—Children rise. Bible reading and prayer. Daddy goes to work. Breakfast.

7:30—Dress, make beds, etc.

8:00—Chores. Charity does the dishes. Abby and Priscilla each milk our two Guernsey cows. We always have milk to spare, and often butter and whipped cream. Eve feeds our few calves. They live outside in a little pen.

We have thirty or more pigs altogether. Naomi and Luke tend to them. Sometimes their food is stuck in the feeder and they must poke it to get it going again.

I start the wash, or bread or cleaning. Then for grades two to eight, the understanding is that they read directions and do the assignment. If they run into trouble, they are free to come to me wherever I am. Their schedules run about like this:

9:00—Prayer and singing.

9:15—Math.

10:15—Recess.

10:30—English, reading and spelling.

12:00—Lunch and recess.

1:00—Bible.

2:00—Break.

2:15—Geography and history, one semester; science and government, second semester.

3:15—School's out. Play time. Take turns for piano practice until chore time at 5:00.

6:00—Supper. Dishes—Naomi. I mark papers, etc.

I keep the kindergartener and first-grader downstairs near me and I spend most of the day, off and on, with them. For example,

I sit down with Luke from nine-fifteen until recess. After recess I get him started working by himself, take Hope with me to do a load of wash or some housework, check on him occasionally, fix lunch and check his work.

If he's tired after lunch break he might nap or rest an hour. Then we spend another hour working together. I mark his work as we go, which gives him a chance to make corrections while the problems are fresh in his mind.

I mark the other kids' work during noon hour and rest time so that after school or at night I have only an hour of work. (The first year, I spent at least two hours after supper every night, marking and planning. Home study improves with age!)

I think that one of the first things any mother teaching her children at home must come to terms with is that *you can't do everything.* I'm not "Superwoman." You're not "Superwoman." Dr. Raymond Moore tells me a half day of teaching is enough, so we are now planning more manual activities, e.g., tapping maple trees to make syrup.

There are still only twenty-four hours in every day. The sun sets, the moon climbs across the sky and the sun rushes up again. Your whole schedule starts over again . . . and again . . . and again.

If you spend a few hours a day with schoolwork, marking papers and all else involved, something is going to slide—and it's usually the housework. But children are a big help!

Everyone has to eat, so one fixes three good meals. (In fact, I *began* baking bread on a regular basis during the first year.) And now we have a homeful of bakers.

And clothes must be kept clean. Laundry . . . an endless parade! But it is not meaningless. You should see my assistants!

Youngsters can indeed be quite helpful in this area. Our children (except the two-year-old) make their beds. They each have a laundry bag hanging in their closets, which helps keep their rooms neat and saves a lot of time and steps. When I'm ready to wash, I just say, "Bring down your dirty clothes bags," and that's a big help.

I think it would be most helpful if some of these routines could be fairly well established before school starts. It's hard to begin all routines at the same time.

And by all means, set some priorities. I determined beforehand, there were two things I would not neglect: a normal baby-childhood for the preschoolers and the family-together-after-suppertime in the living room. As a result, I think Hope got more cuddling than the rest! And I discovered that it's perfectly possible to mark papers, etc., in the midst of piano practicing, puzzle-fixing, newspaper reading or the rest.

After two years of home study we still don't have all the answers. Neither do the regular schools, however, though they often pretend to.

Abby still hasn't friends her age. And our friends just didn't have babies that year! She substitutes with younger and older girls and doesn't complain, but we're not satisfied and are searching. Yet we are realizing more and more that we, their parents, must be their best friends. This worked in the old days. Why not now?

I'm still exhausted too much of the time. September is a month for finishing up canning peaches, tomatoes, etc., as well as starting school. A family of nine just plain involves a lot of work, even with shortcuts and cooperation. That may ease up or solve itself in time as each year does seem to improve. But I am learning to transfer jobs, and the kids do well.

We still run into administrative snags. The wrong book is sent and we must wait a while for the right one, but it's nothing insurmountable.

On the positive side we enjoy the program. The kids far prefer it to regular school. Maybe it's not perfect, but oh so good!

"I have more time to do things I want around the farm because we don't spend time going from home to school and back again," Abby says. "I like reading and crocheting."

Naomi echoes her. "I like our textbooks better than those we had before and I like studying by myself. I study as much as I did before but because our home is school we still have time for extra things."

The initial cool reaction of a lot of acquaintances is warming up. We get suggestions for field trips, books and teaching aids. And the rivalry and ridicule of school is absent here.

From the start we've recognized that all learning isn't from books so we take trips to the zoo, the museum, etc. All the kids are avid readers so we stock up on books from the local library every other week. And we learn a lot from work!

I can't say that our home school has strikingly changed our kids' behavior because they were generally well-behaved and good students to begin with.

We hope that their values have benefited but that's often hard to judge until later. However, one incident points up the general direction.

Upon hearing rock music at a friend's house, our timid daughter spoke up against it and quietly left. The friend called her up and chose her companionship over the music. You can imagine how she felt! I just don't think this would have happened two years ago.

Our children's attitude toward their home study has been positive since the initial adjustment. But it grows more and more so.

"Look at all those *poor* kids riding the bus," they'll laugh, or feel genuinely sad for them.

After a particularly good and enjoyable art lesson, Abby glows and says, "I guess we're not so deprived after all!" We tend to joke about the reaction of some, that the kids are neglected, mistreated or deprived.

Priscilla, especially, is artistic. She has a good eye for detail and isn't happy unless her drawing suits her critical view. Her horses actually look like horses! Mine don't.

Three of the girls enjoy musical instruments. Abby had taken a year of flute lessons and had one year in band before we began home study. She keeps up with it and improves by regular practice.

Naomi began taking cornet lessons this summer and Priscilla is broadly hinting that an instrument would be a *wonderful* gift for her November birthday.

Most of them take and practice piano regularly and we've given a couple of "band concerts" to Daddy and other family.

As an example of our extra-curricular activities, last fall we had some neighbor children and friends over for a husking bee by a bonfire. The fire warmed our bodies and spirits and burned up an eyesore heap of junk. We followed the husking bee with refreshments and a spelling bee.

Some wonder when the children will return to conventional schools. That depends on several factors.

The Academy offers coursework through the twelfth grade. If the subject matter gets too heavy for me to handle in addition to my full-time mother tasks, we would not be so foolish as to let their education suffer just to keep them home. On the other hand, the teacher's manuals have been excellent and we don't anticipate any problems.

If they desire to go to college—and the older ones have already indicated this—we'll decide together where they will attend.

In summary, the few problems of home-school—the early opposition, the extra time it takes to supervise and correct papers, even our legal battle—have been far outweighed by the value to us of educating our children at home.

Perhaps the greatest value is that we have grown to think of everything in terms of family. Functioning as a unit, instead of nine individuals who happen to use the same house, is very rewarding.

It carries over from school work to their cheerfully working together to painting the trim on the house, to canning vegetables, to preparing for picnics.

This unity and teamwork—instead of making the kids reserved and withdrawn—has given them the confidence and independence that comes from realizing their value as part of our family and children of God.

EIGHT

The Oil Man and the Housewife*
———————with Marie Gray———————

When we decided to keep Kevin out of school until he was eight and one half, we didn't anticipate any problems with school and state officials and we didn't have any. Our son was happy enough to remain home even though his two best friends were beginning then at age seven. We told him that we would be able to travel more, and do many more fun and interesting things at home than the children in school could do.

We did take some minor precautions, however, mainly explaining our plan to our nearest neighbors so they would understand why seven-year-old Kevin worked and played around our two hundred acre farm instead of spending his days in a classroom. One neighbor, a former elementary school teacher, liked the idea and thought we'd made a wise decision.

Yet, we met opposition in surprising places, from friends and members of our church. The first grade teacher of our church school strongly felt that we were making a mistake in keeping him out. She had twenty-five years of teaching experience behind her and could see no benefit of his starting at a later age.

Some felt we were "radical." Others could not comprehend the importance we placed on letting Kevin's mind and muscles

---

*All names for this chapter have been changed at the request of the author.

mature and his coordination develop before confining him to a desk and putting a small pencil in his little hand. We also deemed of great importance his emotional development and feelings of self-worth before exposing him to the classroom community. We sought to teach him our values, giving him a firm spiritual foundation and awareness of God as his Friend and Companion before his secular training began.

For all these reasons, and more, we kept him home while his six and seven-year-old neighbors went to school. We considered our home a school, anyway. We thought the widely varied experiences offered on our Missouri farm and with his daddy were an important part of our boy's education, too.

Unlike many farm families, our mornings do not begin too early because neither Frank nor I work away from the home, except for Frank's trips as an energy and minerals specialist. Following breakfast and morning worship, Kevin had chores around the farm. Pets needed caring for, calves must be fed, the cows and horses had to be watered. At first he stretched his short legs to match Frank's longer ones, and son followed the father model in learning to care for the animals. Before long Kevin, at age seven, could do it alone.

He has always been a self-confident boy and at age seven decided he wanted to buy a calf. Going to livestock auctions with us was nothing new but one day the event held more than normal excitement. For that day Frank announced that Kevin would bid on and buy a calf. He did the bidding himself with a man bidding against him for awhile. Then the man stopped and Kevin bought the calf for seven dollars and fifty cents. The high spirits of our boy were almost overwhelming: His very own calf which he himself had chosen and bought with his own money!

At first he fed the calf on a bottle but soon it grew larger, its legs grew stronger and it obviously needed more than a liquid diet. So Kevin put it out to pasture where it grazed with the other animals.

With much interest and pride our son watched his little calf grow bigger and bigger. We talked about the fact that the calf was a steer and eventually must be sold. It was with some sadness and a strong sense of accomplishment that two years later he sold his investment for a little over four hundred dollars.

Of course Kevin had small duties around the house, too. He helped with the dishes and kept his room clean. I let him help cook and bake. We found that when children are young, "helping" is exciting, and learning the skills that keep a home running comes easily, without the child even realizing that he's learning anything. He's just enjoying himself. But the key is that he is working with *you!*

After the noon meal I sat down and read to him every day. Kevin loved it but somehow never asked to read for himself. Since Frank's work takes him to many cities away from home, we traveled extensively with him. This was another key reason for our family school. I imagine that Kevin has been to the Oklahoma City Zoo more than a lot of children who live in the area! That is education, too.

He began accordion lessons on his eighth birthday. This is a little early by some estimates, but since he requested this, without our suggesting it, we took a chance. At eleven, he still takes lessons and his teacher thinks he's done exceptionally well. He plays for our enjoyment, for church programs and for the young peoples' visits to nursing homes.

During the summer before he started regular school, I ordered phonics material from Rod and Staff Publishers in Crockett, Kentucky, and reviewed him in phonics. He was a late bloomer in reading. Still we enjoyed our extra year with Kevin at home. We knew that he'd grown emotionally and mentally as well as physically. But by the time he reached eight and a half, we felt the time ready for him to attend school.

We chose a church-related private school, and requested to begin Kevin in the second grade. And that's where the problems began.

The teacher, with her "lifetime of experience" to rely on, insisted that Kevin enter the first grade. And we—his parents, the ones closest to him and most aware of his abilities—were sure that he should begin in the second. Frank and I were aware of the research and work of Raymond and Dorothy Moore at the Hewitt Research Foundation and of their findings that most children who begin school at a later age are wholly capable of working with their peers, and, in fact, of excelling.

A sad example, with which we were acquainted, added to our determination. Parents of another bright little boy had kept him out past the usual starting age. When he began, they placed him in the first grade. From the beginning he didn't fit in because he was older and larger than his classmates. Yet the adults who ruled his life couldn't see that boredom and inability to fit in with his classmates contributed to his problems. They made him stay with children younger than he grade after grade, until he became cast in a backward role and now could not escape it. We would not let that happen to Kevin.

Frank and I took our unusual request to the school board and the local education leader. However we hadn't considered our request unusual and hadn't realized the furor we would cause. It seemed that they actually didn't know what to do with us. They suggested that perhaps Kevin might skip a grade later on, say the sixth or seventh, if he proved himself capable. Then they said he would be "caught up."

When we insisted on starting our boy at least in the second grade, for many his age were in the third, the education leader told us that if we were so critical of the school's way of handling children perhaps we should enroll Kevin somewhere else. We were tempted to feel hurt. We had chosen this school because we felt it offered a high quality education with more individual attention to the students. During this time I contacted Dorothy Moore and asked her counsel. Mrs. Moore knew of other parents in the same situation who had allowed themselves to be intimidated and their children kept back.

With her encouragement we decided to tactfully talk with the teachers again. We pointed out to the teacher that Kevin could at least do second-grade work. The teacher's classroom consisted of grades one through four, and she finally agreed that Kevin could begin in grade two *if* he also did most of the first-grade work.

And so, with that compromise, Kevin began school. He was happy in the grade with his special friends, and although the teacher and principal had reservations, we were satisfied and confident.

We, Kevin's parents, couldn't change their minds but Kevin could. And he did. Academically he has passed even our expectations. He has good study habits, socializes well and is highly motivated. His teacher kept him busy doing the first grade workbooks—unfairly, we believed—but he completed them so easily and so well (in addition to his regular second grade work) that it became obviously unnecessary. It is remarkable how the teacher changed her opinion of late starters when she saw how well Kevin did in comparison with the other students.

Before Kevin started school I gave both the teacher and the principal a copy of one of the Moore's books, *Better Late Than Early,* but neither seemed interested in reading it.

Last year Dr. Moore spoke at a teachers' convention which our teachers attended. One of his lectures included his research and discoveries on early childhood education, and apparently had its effect. Later Kevin's teacher told me, "When I got home from the convention I called my daughter and begged her not to send her son to school next year. He's the regular age to begin right now."

When the principal and his wife returned from the convention, their minds were completely changed in regard to school entrance age. His wife remarked to me that they only wished they'd been open-minded enough to have read *Better Late Than Early* when I had offered it to them. They also mentioned how easy it was to understand after hearing Dr. Moore's presentation.

As for us, we are proud of Kevin and happy with his achievements. I'm sure that at school he has been influenced by his peers in some ways that cut across our ideals for him. Yet he gets along unusually well with both children and adults.

Kevin is now eleven and in the fifth grade. My only regret now is that we sent him to formal school at all. There is a lot of plain foolishness in the classroom, so much wasted time. On occasion when Kevin has had to stay home, he has completed his actual schoolwork in an hour and one-half. "If it takes you only an hour and one-half to do your lessons," I asked him, "what do you do for the rest of the day in school?"

"Well—"

Of course I realize that teacher presentation and class discussion involves time. Yet it seems such a waste of our childrens' hours. Kevin brings these habits into our home life too so that time has less meaning than before. There's a lack of Christian refinement in the classroom, even in our small school. Of course this goes back to how his classmates are trained in their homes. Yet it influences Kevin in *our* home.

There is far too much emphasis on rivalry sports and the "win at any cost" attitude that goes with it. We'd rather Kevin value himself for the way he has developed his God-given abilities, and to help those who are less able than he, rather than competing with his peers. The result of all this excitement is that our son gets little sound help in music and other enriching experiences. Self-worth developed by the child who recognizes his value as an able worker and who helps others seems to us far more important than the pride a child feels in himself because he can kick a ball higher than his smaller, less muscular classmates.

We also have a younger son Teddy, who will be eight next September. He also has stayed home as Kevin did. However, we plan to teach Teddy at home next year, beginning his work on the level most suited to his needs and abilities. We are strongly considering teaching Kevin at home also.

We feel there is an urgent need for parents to realize the value of allowing their children to mature physically and emotionally beyond the arbitrary six years set by today's educators—an age that, for most children, contradicts sound research. And after that, there is a need within the school system for teachers to tailor their program to the late-starters who have already learned basics at home. My heart still goes out to our young friend whose parents started him late—crippled by "the system." What his parents sought to accomplish was largely undone by teachers and a school board who did not know how to deal with him. We pray for teachers trained in how to deal effectively with the student who begins school later, and how to work practically with students when they do go to school.

NINE

The Dentist and the Nurse
—————————with Rosemary Sprague—————————

To tell our story of home school means to share our values and tell of our life style—something very personal to us. I am a thirty-five-year-old mother of three children—Polly Sue (ten); Jennifer (eight); and Gregory (two). My husband, Howard, is a dentist. My degree is in nursing and I have taken subjects in education.

When Polly was four, we never dreamed that she wouldn't go to school at "the regular age" of six. However, when her sixth year did come around, we were impressed to ask permission to keep her out until she was seven. We felt that with the added physical and mental maturity of that extra year, she'd simply have an edge on learning.

During that year we read the *Reader's Digest* book *Better Late Than Early*, the dream of a home school budded, and our lives were changed. Our minds were heavy with the awareness of how much we had at stake—not only for Polly but for Howard and me as well. We found the evidence for home school overwhelming and came to feel strongly that it was our privilege as well as responsibility to educate our children ourselves. So, after mulling it over separately, discussing it together, reading about home education and praying about it, Howard and I decided to make teaching our children our central family activity. We would even relocate to carry out this God-given privilege if the state gave us any problem.

We decided to approach the issue head on and so, with the school material in hand, we visited our assistant public school superintendent. He was cordial and we appreciated his receptiveness and helpfulness. He copied our material to show his chief, and we left his office with a cautious optimism.

Though they approved of our home program in spirit, their official answer had to be "no" because of the, said they, New Hampshire law. They had no authority to give approval to our program (although we understand some states leave interpretation of the law to the local schools). We then contacted a lawyer who agreed to represent us and help us work out a solution. All this we accomplished without malice, acquiring new acquaintances and sharing *Better Late Than Early* with others.

But, alas, eventually we received two notices from the assistant school superintendent stating that Polly must be enrolled by a certain date or we would be subject to prosecution. Of course we were concerned but managed to weather this stressful four weeks. Howard dealt with the pressure, talking with our lawyer, etc. Me? During this time intravenous feeding was helping me cope with my third pregnancy.

My Aunt Olive stayed with us weekdays for ten weeks until I could resume my duties. We trusted God to help us through, earnestly believing that we were doing the best for our family.

Then the school lawyer and our lawyer found a legal loophole and brought us a possible solution. If we could register Polly at a church school (twenty-four miles away) and if they allowed us to teach at home, it would be considered their affair. We'd meet the letter of the law and Polly would be registered in a state-approved school.

And do you know, it worked! Our home school was treated as a satellite to the church school. We were so grateful to the lawyers for working to help us and to God who led them to the solution.

This is our fourth year under the umbrella of the church school at Estabrook. Our home school has flowered to include as much as we'd hoped, and has brought us inner satisfaction.

I enjoy my work as their teacher—the girls' dark ponytails bent over their books, the bright happiness when they "catch on" to a hard problem, Polly helping Jennifer with something she's already mastered. And these are the Christian growth sessions when stormy attitudes have to be identified and dealt with using Jesus principles. Our angels have some dark rings in their halos! I treasure these moments as jewels to be saved and guarded. We share moments of closeness impossible in a home where the children spend most of their waking hours away. Often we sense a warmth about our little "classroom," an intangible glow, elusive, impossible to catch and keep but nevertheless real.

Polly and Jennifer (now in grades five and two) take their achievement tests at Estabrook. During the year I report school grades and the number of school days to them. We use Home Study Institute courses which give detailed instruction in all nine areas of study: reading, handwriting, math, social science, health science, language, music and art appreciation, Bible, spelling and physical education. With Home Study, I do the teaching and only mail in the tests for them to correct. They also ask for several projects a period. This usually includes two pieces of art, a map and several written articles.

Our school year is divided into six periods. Our Home Study teacher can be reached by telephone and letter for assistance. She relates to the girls through letters that compliment, encourage and direct, birthday cards, a photograph now and then, and attractive stickers on their graded tests.

Our Home Study Institute costs run about $300.00 a year per child. I estimate that the expenses for teaching at home are equal to a private school because in my situation I must hire help to keep up with the housework.

We started our venture conscientiously, getting two school desks for the girls, a 4 × 6 chalkboard, a homemade bulletin board and a bookcase. Our adaptable room happened to be near the entryway where everyone passes. I have spent many hours teaching Polly from the sofa, feeding baby Greg on my lap. And you know, it's rewarding and can even be relaxing—the baby in my arms and my little girl studying nearby.

As our classroom evolved, the girls would work at the kitchen table when I cooked or cleaned in the kitchen. This seemed a natural solution and we eventually removed their desks from the "school room" because they rarely used them.

At first I felt that the girls should not be in town during school hours but the demands of life refused to comply. Soon we were comfortable being asked by a friendly saleslady, "Are you playing hooky from school?" The reply that mom teaches us at home brings many different responses! Often we are able to share our unique philosophy of education with people who are interested and who express their wishes for our continued success.

We feel that beyond the benefits of close contact between parents and child in the home school, and the self-esteem which develops as the child becomes aware of her own value without the normal classroom competition and comparison with peers, are the strong points of (1) flexibility, (2) practical improvisation, and (3) creativity.

Flexibility. School can be taught in many different situations. Whether going to town or going on a trip, I have a book for each girl. We often study while traveling in the car, waiting in offices, waiting for Howard, and so on.

Practical improvisation. Polly and Jennifer's handwriting practice is mostly done in the form of correspondence—letters to pen pals and relatives, including thank-you notes. Which, by the way, is necessary etiquette, taught more by experience than by reading rules in a book. We also play math and spelling games for short intervals as we travel.

Physical education has room for great variety. During the fall one of our family projects is splitting and stacking seven to eight cords of wood—physical education of the most basic kind. After we inherited a palomino horse, the girls took horseback riding lessons three times a week for two months. Together we go hiking, cross-country and downhill skiing, and the girls take swimming lessons at the community center. We're much happier with this togetherness form of physical education than with the competition and stress of winning at all costs that we see in many playground situations.

Creativity. Though Howard is unable to take on teaching Polly and Jennifer their regular subjects, he shares just about everything he knows. And the girls are delighted. They learned the Morse code with him, for example. They watch and learn as he takes photographs and develops them in his darkroom. He's interested in astronomy, so they share his excitement in viewing the stars and planets through our fourteen-inch telescope. Howard also plays violin with Polly. In other words, he spends a lot of time with them.

As a family we visit museums, and national parks. We attend concerts and travelogues and films such as Audubon. We would probably attend such programs even if we didn't have a home school, but our awareness of them as learning tools has been increased.

Because of our lifestyle, school must function around the office where I fill in occasionally. Then there is seasonal work and lots of company, and the needs of the day. At age ten, Polly is my right hand in the kitchen and I am happy to do the less exciting jobs while she develops the art of cooking. When neighbors or friends get sick, Polly gets out the cookbooks to find something to fix for them. We are finding that doing things for needy people in our community is a very special experience for our girls—a very maturing one.

Education is high on our list of priorities, but because of the way we live, we are unable to keep pace with the conventional school hours or schedules. Our school work, however, is accomplished easily within a calendar year and achievement is good. Besides the three R's, we want the children to learn principles that will guide them in correct decision-making. I have a feeling that our appreciation for God will correlate to our appreciation for each other. So appreciation and respect for people and property rank high in our minds.

Because I cannot sing accurately, I have not sung to our children. Their music experience has been with records, concerts, church and private lessons. Polly began piano lessons at age six and did so well and happily with them, that we started her on the violin at age seven, possibly a little sooner than is best. Her violin lessons included a beginners' orchestra. Six months ago she wanted to begin the cello so now she alternates violin and cello lessons. Perhaps it would be difficult to work in enough time for practice after a conventional school day, but with home study and our flexible schedule there is little or no problem. Polly dreams of being a music teacher and we have been thankful for the gifted, Christian music teachers who are working with her.

In keeping with the research concerning the benefits of reading to young children, I started my personal reading aloud to Polly before she was two years old. Reading aloud has become a tradition for us. Rarely do the children go to bed without our reading to them and on trips we literally have reading marathons. Our usual subjects are Bible stories and other true stories, biographies and nature books.

When Polly was four I read a biography of Florence Nightingale to her, which included the problem of her extreme shyness. After hearing this, Polly confided that she had the same fears and feelings. This insight helped me to understand her behavior and gradually, through simple errands and everyday encounters, Polly has gained control of her shyness.

Home school has taught me my limits. I can't go here and there on a whim, and I must say no to many things that I once enjoyed. Often there is not time for activities that I want to do. Adequate sleep is an essential part in keeping up our program and this too is hard for me. Some say we are doing too much for our children, and that is probably so. We are learning as we go. I mention these things only because I want to be realistic in what I share about our home school. I'd hate for anyone to begin teaching their children at home without being totally committed and aware of the limits that it sets upon one's time and the problems that can arise. Also I'd be less than honest if I pretended that I'm completely self-sufficient. My mother and my Aunt Olive help me in so many ways.

After sharing these problems, I must hurry to add that I am thankful for the privilege of working with our children and for the responsibility I feel toward them. It isn't a sacrifice, for the rewards are much greater than the efforts would suggest. I wouldn't do it any other way. Howard is with us, giving his total support and time whenever possible, also helping to guide and discipline the children. Without his encouragement, I doubt that I could continue.

Since our children have grown up sitting through meetings and listening to stories, it is easy to keep their attention. For school we simply open a book and work together.

The girls are only twenty-two months apart in age, yet there are three grades between them. Polly tends, as I said, to be shy and Jennifer is just the opposite. Polly is musical and reads everything around her. When using the encyclopedia she's easily distracted from her topic by other subjects. While putting away cans, she's reading the labels.

In contrast, Jennifer is very active, concerned with the temporal, and has a gift for socializing. She was seven and a half before she started piano—which we now understand may still be too young, according to surveys of professional music teachers. She continues to take piano but her favorite activity is gymnastics. She recently started gymnastic lessons with a private teacher and in turn teaches Polly and even little Greg. Our bedroom has become a gym and our king size bed has become a trampoline, though we do not allow it to get too wild.

From my childhood, I know how important pets are. They aid the imagination and help in acting out childhood fantasies. Our family horse, unmatched in gentleness and beauty, wins many blue ribbons in their minds. Their four rabbit friends have kept the girls pulling grass and dreaming all summer.

Polly and Jenny love to make doll clothes. With scrap material and Grandma's button collection they have designed and sewn wardrobes for their twenty small dolls.

Together we are sewing wrap-around skirts for the girls. They have shown an interest in rug braiding so we are planning the colors for the bedroom rug they will make. We are thinking that this hobby may develop into something profitable before long.

We plan for the children each to learn dental assisting and office management in Howard's office when they are teen-agers. This will give them practical appreciation for business courses and a profession that they can use.

There is no end to creative ideas but there is a limit to my time, patience and energy. Since the children go everywhere with us, I have little time to myself. One refreshing spot in the day is my 7:30 A.M. two-mile walk with a neighbor. I would suffer, particularly during the confining winter months, without this exercise, for it clears my mind and gives me energy to begin my work.

We had a rewarding experience this year in sharing our home with a thirteen-year girl from Japan. Her maturity, discipline and courage inspired us all. The LABO Program, which she was with, did an excellent job of preparing us for her visit. The month flew by, the time passing far too quickly, and the good-byes of our new friend left us with a desire to learn more about other cultures. We are hoping to have a girl from another country next year.

My latest idea concerns helping the girls learn a second language. We have a connection with a family of girls of corresponding ages in Austria. By exchanging our girls on alternate summers we will both benefit and our girls will be able to talk and even think in German. We believe this exchange of cultures and languages invaluable as all peoples are truly a part of God's family.

Today, Sunday, we all worked at the church and office for six hours. It is 9:30 P.M. Howard has just returned from overseeing a clinic to help people stop smoking.

Polly, Jennifer and I have been doing school work for the last two hours. Mostly I have been listening to Jenny read. While I listened, Polly practiced her music, and two-year-old Greg kept quietly amused by cutting paper into a hundred pieces over the rug. Now the children are practicing gymnastics on our bed. And so our school without bells somehow continues to bring harmony and fun to our home.

TEN

The Teacher and the Dairy Man
——————————with Lenora Blank——————————

A knock at the door momentarily hushed the cadence of voices within.

"Welcome! We're waiting to get started," Doug Ort greeted Henry and Carol Foote.

Six sets of parents were now gathered in the country living room. Mothers' ears were half-tuned to the low sounds of primary-aged children playing in another room. "It's thrilling," Doug observed as he sat down, "that the principles of the Bible preached by the apostles and the reformers can still have direct application even to the education of our children today!"

Trenton Frost agreed. "We, as parents, have exactly that privilege and responsibility."

Henry nodded too. "Everything," he gestured broadly, "has a practical correspondence both to this life and in eternity when God again intervenes in human history."

"Well," interjected practical Sara Ort, "let's see how that translates into educational content, method, and setting!"

I seconded Sara, and Jim Foote added, "Lenora, you're our teacher-in-chief." With that, Lenora called the meeting to order.

What was happening? What would the outcome be?

The year, 1974.

The place, Canton, New York.

It started the day Douglas Ort hung up the telephone, a troubled expression on his face.

He would tell his wife immediately, but should they tell five-year-old Dougie? Yes, he decided, for Dougie's at the heart of the problem—a situation that the Orts had expected to avoid for another year.

Mr. Meldrum, the local elementary school principal, had just said in essence that "though Douglas will not be six until November 15, his birthday comes before the cut-off date of December 1, and New York law requires him to be in school."

School had been in session for one week. For one week, five-year-old Dougie had been an innocent truant. Neither of the Orts were teachers. Doug was a preacher by calling and worked to support the family as a Dairy Herd Improvement Supervisor. Sarah was an occupational therapist, and a mother of four pre-school-aged children.

The Orts asked for and were granted an appointment with Mr. Meldrum to discuss some ideas with him before their son entered the first grade. This situation now forced them, along with five of our other like-minded families with eleven children between the ages of two and five—to come to grips with a question we'd hoped to delay. We had strong reservations against starting our children in school at the usual age of six, preferring to wait until they were at least eight years old.

Nor were we comfortable with the public school education and what it was doing with many children socially, morally and academically. We wanted to guide our children into a total education not only as citizens of earth's society but also as children of God.

We talked among ourselves a good deal and agreed on an awareness of our role under a loving Heavenly Father. God must be the foundation to all education—mental, physical, spiritual and social.

But we needed permission to develop and implement our own philosophy of education. We concluded that *life is the best school,* and began to discover the potential of our own homes as the places for "classroom" instruction and practical, everyday living with values we hold dear.

In the days before the Ort's appointment with the principal, Doug made several long-distance phone calls to different attorneys and others whom he thought might provide them with legal advice. Beginning in New York, he discovered that the curriculum used by private schools does not enjoy actual state recognition. As parents trying to teach their children at home it seemed that the state was more concerned with *why* they planned to do so, rather than what they would teach.

He spoke with lawyers well known for their knowledge of religious liberty. He contacted Dr. Raymond Moore of the Hewitt Research Foundation, a recognized educator and developmental psychologist whose research on early childhood education is thoroughly documented and widely known. Dr. Moore gave them a lot of practical help and agreed to provide expert witness if their situation developed into a court trial. He also sent stacks of material presenting the reasons for allowing a child to delay formal schooling until he is physically and emotionally mature.

The Orts were, as yet, unsure about their relationship with Mr. Meldrum and strongly felt their lack of time to prepare their case. They were willing to allow their son to be a test case, if it came to that.

"But we just don't have the money to pay lawyers," Doug's wife Sara told us repeatedly. "We really don't want to cause trouble because of our convictions," she groaned while awaiting the inevitable confrontation with school officials.

It turned out that Mr. Calvin Peterson, the Canton District Superintendent, accompanied Mr. Meldrum when the meeting with Doug and Sarah Ort occurred. All were cordial, but it seemed that they were equally unsure of what the Orts' situation might entail for them.

In this New York dairyland, an area with a lot of miles and a sparse population of low-income families, the school officials knew of people who wanted to keep their children at home simply because they didn't care much about education. The Orts soon realized that Mr. Meldrum and his associate seemed mostly concerned with their *motive* for keeping Dougie home. They were now thankful that they'd done their research and could present sound reasons against sending their five year old to the first grade.

The Orts outlined their philosophy of education and stressed that they were not trying to evade their educational responsibilities but in actuality were concerned for Dougie's best interests, wanting to give him more time to develop at home until he was ready to begin school.

Mr. Peterson and Mr. Meldrum agreed and granted permission to keep Dougie at home until he was eight and would be more ready for formal schooling.

For the first year, Sara created a little set of goals for Dougie, using some of her own ideas and a variety of other preschool materials. The next year, 1975-76, the children of two more families—ours and the Marchants—turned six. My family also made an appointment with Mr. Peterson and requested permission to do as the Orts had done. He thoughtfully and kindly and quickly granted our request.

As the families shared their ideas, the group began to form a more specific outline of instruction for the children. Each set of parents was responsible for its own children's education, but would be working together wherever group action might be more effective and efficient. Every parent, we agreed, would share something for the benefit of all the students.

Because I have a degree in elementary education, they chose me to act as teacher coordinator for those times when the children might be together in a group. Thinking that I would need additional education and current permanent certification, I began to work for a master's degree in education at the State University of New York. Between then and 1977 I began to study more about home schooling and wrote several term papers dealing with this philosophy. My work on them gave us all the opportunity to struggle with and crystallize our personal goals and objectives in home schooling.

In the fall of 1975, we began the home-school program. Sarah Ort and I wanted to do something with the oldest three children in our group—Douglas Ort, David Marchant and my Shari. The children were excited and expectant, yet it seemed difficult for us to get started. Sara and I were just not exactly sure how to complement each other in the nitty-gritty of our first day of school. For we weren't planning now and we weren't theorizing on paper anymore. Suddenly, we had to be teachers. Our little children waited, empty cups anxious to be filled.

So we plunged in. Soon the uncertainties were ironed out; we became comfortable working with each other and with the children. Teaching now seemed as natural and as much of our routine as fixing dinner or telling a bedtime story. School had become a part of everyday life.

Beyond that, the program of 1975–76 evolved into four mothers with similar values meeting with all the youngsters: Sara Ort, Carol Foote, Sherryl Marchant and Dorita Frost. I was taking graduate courses at this time. Altogether there were fourteen children between the ages of three and seven.

We had our own children in our homes, of course. But we often joined to read stories, play records and sing with the children. The group went hiking, viewed library films, and learned Spanish under Dorita's direction. It was amazing how fast even the younger children soaked up Spanish. We made no formal attempt to teach them to read or write it, of course, but they loved singing or rattling off their numbers in Spanish—*uno, dos, tres*—instead of the mundane one, two, three.

It was necessary to have another meeting with our schoolmen, for by 1976–77 David Ort, Melissa Frost and Rachel Foote had turned six. So that fall all of us parents met with Mr. Peterson. We discussed with him then that not only did we want to delay classroom education until age eight, but we wanted to continue teaching our children at home. It was proving to be a rewarding experience to parents and children and our "school" was going very well. Mr. Peterson agreed and turned the operational details over to Mr. Meldrum, who asked for monthly activity reports and attendance records. I gladly provided them.

In 1977–78 the Ort home became the center of the group education. Besides daily teaching the three R's, we taught Bible, social studies, industrial arts and health. Henry Foote held a weekly science class. Trenton Frost, an accomplished artist, taught art and Dorita Frost continued Spanish. When William Blank held monthly astronomy meetings at night, the children were awed by moon craters they viewed through a telescope and they followed our trusty flashlight beaming toward different constellations. They played little games to help them learn the names of the planets in our solar system and several times we watched movies from a local free film service. We regularly used films for various parts of our curriculum.

Jim Foote was nature and hiking leader while his wife helped with choir and cooking. In November, for example, we had several birthdays so decided to have a special dinner. The children planned the menu and helped scrub potatoes, set the table, make the salads and so forth. We held cooking class every week or two. Twice a month Sara ordered free educational films from the library.

This was the hey-day for our group home-school, we parents and our children were totally involved in their work. It was a happy time, a time of sharing and laughter—and learning. Much learning as the students—more physically and emotionally mature than the usual first graders—rapidly advanced at their individual paces through the classwork.

In 1978 and 79 there were changes. The Footes moved away and the Frosts' work schedule and transportation problems made involvement in the group school impossible for them. Seven children remained in the home school.

Meanwhile we faced another problem. Our school officials had willingly cooperated with us for a few years but now several other requests for various alternatives to public education were being brought to Mr. Peterson's attention. Pressure grew for us to put our children in regular school.

Mr. Peterson made the State Education Department aware of what he was confronted with, and then worked with them to create a new set of guidelines for uniform dealings with private schools in the county. They then lumped our home education a "private school." This came as a blow, for we had never thought we fit in that category, yet wanted to meet the requirements. This was a serious threat to us, for private school status involved meeting fire-inspection codes, etc., which applied to public buildings.

The Orts' home wasn't equipped with crash bars, exit signs, stainless steel sinks, etc., and they couldn't afford such a building. Part of the "genius" of our whole program was the low cost involved. Heat and lighting were actually home costs and our new books and materials were averaging not more than fifty dollars per year as we received supplies from a variety of sources.

So we considered all the options we could think of: Home Study Institute, Accelerated Christian Educational Program, Christian Liberty Academy, and others. Happily for us, a lawyer friend unearthed some New York educational laws, regarding precedents already set for parents teaching their children at home. It was just what we needed. We wrote to Mr. Peterson, requesting that we not be considered in any way a private school. We asked instead that each family be regarded as involved strictly in parental education under such laws as applied to parents. He and Mr. Meldrum came to see our home school and our request met with approval. We were thankful to be able to continue another year.

When 1979–80 came, Sara Ort and I, with help from my husband, William, in science, carried the teaching load for the Orts' four children, my daughter, Shari, and Jeremiah Foote. We met together four days a week. However, we also worked separately in our own homes.

By the end of the year, Douglas and Shari had completed the

fifth grade. David, a year younger, had completed all the fifth-grade work but math. John, age eight, finished second grade and started third. Jeremiah, age seven, and Kathy, seven, finished the first grade and started on second grade math.

In August, 1980, the Orts moved to Florida, nearly ending the original group endeavor. Two families—the Blanks and Jim Footes, remain and are working together. Shari Blank, eleven, and Jeremiah Foote, now eight, have individual home programs under their parents' supervision. Sometimes they share activities when they can meet together.

As a sidelight, the Jim Footes' older son, Jimmy, nine, has Down's Syndrome. He is affected but not severely retarded and did well in the home kindergarten-school. All of us found it a surprise and a joy to see what he could accomplish in the friendly, non-threatening atmosphere.

For the children, having Jimmy as a friend—accepting his limitations as they accepted each other's various little problems—was a valuable experience. They became attuned to his special needs but mostly treated him like a "regular fellow." For the past two years, Jimmy has been in a special-education class at the Hermon-Dekalb Central School and his teachers now consider him one of their star pupils.

We believe that home teachers should be constantly trying to improve themselves—not under strain, but alert to opportunities to improve as parents and teachers. We have been fortunate to be living within twenty miles of four colleges and universities. The State University at Potsdam has a large number of curriculum and learning devices which we could borrow for a semester at a time. We researched New York State requirements for each grade and as we became familiar with what was needed, each parent either created his own "unit" around a particular concept or followed whatever book seemed to best meet his needs.

We have used a wide range of materials. In reading, for example, our school books include some of the old "Dick and Jane" and "Alice and Jerry" series and a variety of other readers which have sound values, some of them recommended in Dr. Moore's new book, *Home-Grown Kids.*

The parents wrote on the chalkboard sentences that the children had just spoken—to enable each child to both hear and see what they had said. Then cards with the words on them became a part of a personal file for each child.

The length of school time has grown as the children became older, beginning with one to two hours twice a week, to four hours a day, four times a week. While the "official" hours spent in group sessions have been less than in regular school settings, they had many constructive manual jobs to do. And all the children always completed a year's worth of schoolwork well before the school year was out.

We teachers figured out what work needed to be covered in a certain amount of time and created goal sheets so the older children could plan and record their daily progress in relation to weekly and yearly goals. Often they would motivate themselves, deciding what they needed to do, and parents just worked as advisors.

We found one of the beauties of the home schedule is its flexibility, yet the students were able to use their "goal sheets" as a framework and work within them.

School officials at one time seemed a little worried. After all, the law required that our youngsters be in school.

"You can see, of course, that they aren't very neglected," Doug Ort reminded them.

"Yes, but . . ." Mr. Meldrum and Mr. Peterson had State guidelines to meet. They were certainly kind enough in view of these pressures. Clearly they were more concerned about the welfare of the children than the letter of the law.

"What do you suggest?" Doug inquired.

"It would be wise to test them, see how they compare with others of their ages."

"What tests do you have in mind?"

"The Stanford Achievement Tests are given each year to public school students in our area," he said.

"Well, let's give them to our youngsters, too."

We parents administered the tests and were excited by the results. We knew our children were happy and content. We knew that they both studied and worked well, but we had not realized how well. Dougie finished the third grade in the 99th percentile at age nine. David Ort finished the second grade in the 96th percentile at eight. Shari Blank, age nine, scored in the 94th percentile on these Stanford Achievement Tests.

Two third-graders and one second-grader finished in the 90th percentile and the tests showed that another little girl had covered two years in one, in reading.

We decided not to pat ourselves on the backs when we saw these scores, but to thoughtfully consider what methods were working best so we could continue using them.

The children are often asked "Where do you go to school?" and their reply, "I go to Home School," has brought many questions. Soon they realized that their situation carries a certain uniqueness and have developed a keen sense of self-identity in dealing with those questions. The children really enjoy their home school. Not that they couldn't have been happy in other situations, but they wouldn't want the opportunity they've had to be taken from them. As my daughter, Shari, begged me, "Please don't write about us for Dr. Moore if it means we can't have home school!"

In contact with other families outside of the schoolroom, the children have opportunities to meet a number of other children. Some of these are students in either public or private schools and comparisons or differences in lifestyles are part of the conversation. However, they seem to have little difficulty in accepting one another and in finding ways to enjoy their time together.

The children are not perfect. They have their squabbles and sibling rivalries at times. They need correction and direction as all children do, yet there are certain qualities about them that are refreshing. They enjoy simple, natural things in diet and play. They create all kinds of pioneer set-ups, etc., from materials around their premises and role-play happily together for hours. When motivated, they work quickly and harmoniously together at a job such as filling the wood box or mulching the garden. They love to read and are happy in their lessons, free from the pressures of competition.

For other parents contemplating home education, we make these suggestions.

Develop your own philosophy of education based on your convictions. Study the right books and if necessary, contact home-school experts.

Consider the cost, which includes time, courage and a little money. You may only be teaching an hour and a half to two hours a day formally, but school includes everything you do.

You may be able to start without contacting school authorities. We found it best to seek local educational approval when we began teaching at home. If you take this route, be able to clearly explain what you want to do and why. Be able to state your curriculum and know where you can get materials. Be aware of what laws regarding alternative education exist in your state.

There is a great lack of uniformity in dealing with a new home-school situation. Some have found public school superintendents who would just as soon "let sleeping dogs lie." Some parents have been told, "If we didn't know about you, we wouldn't have to enforce the laws against you."

If you are able to conduct your home school under the umbrella of your local school—as a satellite of that school—that can save you many unnecessary problems. There is no reason to enter your home-education program with your boxing gloves on.

Although disadvantaged, even a single parent can successfully manage a home school. Not even a college education is mandatory—though recommended. Remember that several of us in Canton did not have college degrees, and those of us who did were in different academic areas. Simply being good home models and demonstrating that your children received adequate instruction (and more) can establish you as a home educator.

We began home school because we felt the need for our children. We continue it now because it is still working as the best option in our circumstances. Frankly, we'd miss the closeness, and the chance to witness the total development of our children if it were any other way.

ELEVEN

The Florida Revelation

―――――――――with Donna Brinkle―――――――

I didn't set out to be a militant mother, the kind who would move heaven and earth and challenge judges and school principals to insure that my kids got a good education. I was just an average Florida housewife, a conscientious wife and mother. A good citizen. I supported the PTA, the school open house and helped with the yearly carnival.

Until the movie, that is.

A friend asked me to go to a movie and exhibit concerning sex education in the public schools. I was interested, even curious. I'd always liked to be involved in what concerned my family. That evening changed our lives.

I realized later that I had been so concerned with helping to purchase the modern teaching equipment that I had not once considered *what* was being taught. I admit I was shocked. The philosophy of sex education and the libertine approach to society that I saw there shook me to the core. I didn't want that favorably taught to my sons.

Joe, my husband, shared my concern and so we put our two younger boys in a small, local church school. Tenth-grade Richard had to continue in public school because the new school went only to the ninth grade. Young Joel, who had just finished the sixth grade, thought we were grossly unfair to snatch him out of his public-school social life and stick him in a little school. But drugs were such a problem in his proposed junior high that we didn't even consider letting him go there. I believe few parents realize the peer pressure at this age to indulge in drugs and sex and alcohol, unless the whole school is oriented to higher morals and a more altruistic lifestyle.

Paul entered first grade in the new school and loved it from the start, while Joel continued his protests against the quiet, well-organized atmosphere. But school is for learning—and for friends—and Joel eventually gave in and enjoyed it too.

Two years passed. My husband, Joe, was transferred to central Florida and private school became too expensive. As much as we hated to change, private school was out of the question, so the boys returned to public school.

Paul cried himself through the noisy, overcrowded, permissive third and fourth grades. By the fifth, he didn't cry any more, but my heart cried for him. Although he was never a behavior problem, he didn't seem to be learning well, he couldn't seem to adjust to his new kind of environment, and I often wondered why he *had* to. Was there a way out for him?

But Joel loved the public-school senior high which, incidentally, did not have as serious a drug problem as his other junior high. Somehow those two years in a church school coupled with our religious home-training gave him a personal sense of worth. He no longer felt an overpowering urge for the peer approval which often went against his values, though we still sensed his inner tug-of-war between the two very different value systems.

Throughout this time, we were still concerned with the humanistic philosophy that undergirded the public-school education. We had seen its effect on our oldest son, Richard. We had been affected by his rebellion and endured the hectic years before he returned to the teachings of his childhood. We were concerned with his self-centeredness and lack of respect for authority. He viewed his parents as his enemies, which is stressed by this philosophy, and all along we were helpless to stop its being taught to him.

Then I discovered Marion Ryan, a mother who, after a long legal battle, discovered a Florida statute which enabled her to form a corporation permitting her to teach her children *at home.* The corporation was formed by a charter requiring the signatures of twenty-five persons, which was then approved and signed by a circuit court judge. Under this charter, parents could join the home-school system and have their own children assigned to them to teach. Parents choose the subjects and pay the costs, making a monthly report to the school on the student's progress. Her school system, however, could only operate within the bounds of the county she lived in and I didn't live in that county.

I was excited by the benefits of teaching the boys at home. If they didn't understand something, they could continue studying it until they mastered it and they could branch out to include areas of special interest. We also could use different textbooks and teach within our philosophy.

Wonderful! I went to the Law Library at the Courthouse for a copy of the Compulsory Education Law and Florida Statute 623, and used these to draft my own charter. I wanted to be prepared if and when I had the courage to make the change.

It was Paul who gave me the final nudge into teaching at home. He brought home a sixth-grade textbook and laughingly said, "Look at the funny things in this book, Mom." I saw a drawing of the stages of monkeys evolving into man. My, this is interesting, I said to myself. I read on to discover that the Communist Revolution was favorably compared to the American Revolution, and there were several other points that shocked me as being contrary to our whole American philosophy of life.

Upset is a mild word for how I felt. I showed the book to Joe and together we wrote a letter to the school principal requesting that Paul be taught from a different book. After writing a detailed book review, I asked to be on the agenda of the next school-board meeting. I went there with high hopes and confidence. Surely these people didn't know what was in that book they had innocently ordered.

I gave them a copy of my book review and presented my case. It was a disaster. I was insulted, criticized, called a book burner and likened to a Nazi. It was a totally useless exercise.

Meanwhile the school principal had decided to put Paul in the library during that class. When Paul got his report card, he received an "0" for the class never attended.

So I, the everyday housewife turned book reviewer, now realized that I had a real contest on my hands. I went to the principal and reminded him that, under the law, Paul was entitled to an education and not a failing grade for a class he could not attend because it violated his conscience. But the principal was not much help.

It became clear to me that we had to start a school of our own. Such a decision is not easy to make—first, fighting the system and then turning your back on it. Could I teach? I wondered. How would Paul and Joel adapt, going from the friends and social life of a busy public school to studying alone on their own?

The boys had to help make this decision too. Richard was graduating and wasn't concerned with home school for himself. He said that he could handle any flack at school caused by what we were trying to accomplish. It wouldn't bother him. Joel too, wanted to stay in public school. That disappointed us, but we respected his decision. Yet later, when our home school was in full swing, he withdrew from public school to study at home. And when he realized that Joe and I weren't going to "give" him a graduating certificate, he buckled down and completed his work, graduating out of our living room. Later he attended college in Idaho.

Meanwhile, Paul stayed in the library during the offending class and I got busy trying to gather the required twenty-five signatures I needed to get a charter for our home school. I was surprised. The people whom I expected to sign for me refused. I asked if they thought parents had the right to teach their own children, if they desired. Many said no, some almost violently.

"Smother mother," one said.

Another warned, "Your kids will be social misfits."

And still another solemnly asked how they could possibly ever adjust to the real world.

Nevertheless, Paul kept track of my progress. "When, Mother, when?"

"As fast as I can, Paul. As fast as I can." I explained over again that we had to have the charter or I could be arrested like Marion Ryan. I wanted to comply totally with the law.

Finally the papers were in order and I set out early to visit every judge in my district. I had to find one who would see me and accept the charter, evaluate it according to the Statute 623, and sign it. Simple, basic legal requirements they were, and I didn't feel like I needed to hire a lawyer to handle such a small chore.

Surprise again! I went to every judge except two, and still did not find one who would handle it. Panic began to flutter in my chest and dry my mouth. Only two judges were left and one of them was on vacation. What could I *do* to convince a judge simply to do what the law said he should do?

The first of these two judges graciously invited me into his chamber. "You must understand that I cannot accept the charter without it being filed and making sure that it has an [attorney's] case number," he told me. A case, I thought. Since when are corporation papers a criminal case?

"But according to Statute 623 it's not necessary for me to have an attorney," I countered. "I understand that all you have to do is to see that the papers are in order with Florida Statute 623."

He looked at me over his glasses as I continued. "I also understand that if a 'case' is made over the issue, there would be a defendant or plaintiff, and a prosecutor. Which would be my position?" I asked him.

"Why, you'd be the defendant and I believe the State Attorney's office would send a prosecutor. Oh yes," he added off-handedly, "and I require a court reporter present at such hearings. You will have to pay for her services."

"But it was my understanding," I replied, "that if the state prosecutes, it usually pays for its own court reporter."

His eyebrows arched. "Oh no, the person who institutes the case has the responsibility of paying this bill."

I didn't answer that, but wheels were spinning in my mind. Interesting, I thought, I'm to pay for my own entrapment. But I had an edge on the judge that he didn't realize. I had been a deputy clerk in Circuit Court and knew the rules and procedures. I knew for one thing that I had the legal right to take my charter and walk out of his court just like I walked in.

"Can you help me expedite this?" I asked him. "Weeks are passing and I want to get on with my school."

He shook his head sadly. "Well, we must get a case number on it first. And it will be three or four weeks before the hearing. I must research the law and go through the legislative records to see what the legislators had in mind when they made the law."

All I could think was, "Poor Paul!" I continued, "But, your Honor, since my charter will be the final instrument and will be recorded it wouldn't be proper, would it, to have a case number stamped all over it?" He graciously asked his secretary to provide me with a cover sheet so a case number could be placed on it. Our meeting over, I went to Recording and paid to have this almost blank sheet of paper filed and a case number affixed to it, making certain that the charter was never marked on. Then I went home to wait.

The phone began to ring as soon as I got in the house. The TV stations wanted to do an interview and the paper was full of stories about the judge's behavior for the next few days. I granted interviews, and most of the reporters treated us fairly, but one story seemed an open invitation for someone to murder us. And every time the case progressed an inch the media was back. On the few occasions we were misquoted, it really hurt. Our church friends would ask us, "Why on earth did you say that!"

"But we didn't say that," we insisted. "They twisted our words."

"But we read it in the paper. We saw it in print."

We had social pressure on all sides against our bucking the system. But on the home front we were united, and that made all the difference.

At one point the judge decided to call in all twenty-five people who signed our charter and have them testify. "You'll have to subpoena them," I told him. "Most of them work, so they would have to get permission from their employers to get off work in order to come in."

Eventually he decided that it wouldn't be necessary to bring them in, but tried other tricks to delay the case. Then he announced that he was going on vacation and his other case load would prohibit him from making a decision in our case until he returned.

It was just the break I had been waiting for.

When I knew he was safely out of town, I went to the courthouse and asked for the case file. It had never been returned to recording where Judge Jones should have sent it, so I asked another judge's secretary if she could get it for me. She was happy to do so.

Next I took my charter out of the file and sent it with a photocopy of Florida Statute 623 to the last possible judge, who had just returned from vacation. He sent word through his secretary that with some minor word changes on the charter, he would be glad to see me and sign it.

I was so excited I could hardly breathe. It seemed too good to be real after all we'd been through. Rushing home, I used my correction fluid and typed in the words he wanted. Then I wrote to the first judge stating that I still had no attorney and to please consider this letter my withdrawal from his court.

On the day of my hearing with the second judge, I hand delivered my withdrawal letter to the recording department, asking that it be clocked in and recorded. Later that day I had the hearing with Judge Murray and walked out of his office with a signed charter which I immediately had recorded. As far as I know, this is the only corporation in Florida that isn't filed at the state level.

I could have danced all the way to Paul's school, but made myself drive over instead and took him out of the library. "He will be attending the Seminole County Private Independent School System, Inc." I told them in the office.

"But we've never heard of that school or a junior high in that locality," they replied.

I tried not to be smug. I was just so happy. "But we do have one there," I told them more gently than I felt, "and that's where he'll be going." Of course they knew me, because of the publicity. We had Paul's permanent records in our hands in three days.

Now what does a mother want to teach her children? How does she determine what has been taught them already? Joel was sixteen when he entered our home school and Paul was eleven. What would Paul need to know before college? Where do you get materials to teach with? and diagnostic tests?

As an aid, I registered our school with the State of Florida and was deluged with advertisements for school materials and supplies. These ads have kept coming through the years.

I went to the public school book depository and they were giving away old books. I came home with a boxload and spread them out—textbooks for classes from the first to twelfth grades—all over my living room floor, I tried to appraise what they taught a child in twelve years. It soon became obvious that any reasonably bright kid should be able to master it all in eight years, but as I thought about it, I knew the reason why. Just think of all the classroom time a child spends waiting while the teacher must help the other students.

To begin, I got a set of McGuffey Readers and gave Paul a whopper of a spelling test. He spelled words until he finally didn't know how to spell most of them, and so that's how we determined his level in spelling.

Multiplication tables? I was in for another surprise. Paul had never learned them because in school the kids used a chart to look up the answers, and they never had to learn them. So Paul graduated to a jar full of dried beans and flash cards. When he counted out seven times seven in beans a few times, the concept impressed itself in his mind, and he found that he could remember. I also tried to devise ways to teach him in which he would discover for himself the answers to various problems. I felt this would build self-confidence, which it did.

Reading was Paul's biggest problem. His permanent school records showed that he had a 3.2 reading-comprehension score at the end of the second grade when he left the Christian school. Tested again at the beginning of the sixth grade, his score was 3.4. In other words, he was at the third-grade, fourth-month level in reading as he was going into the sixth grade. His reading skills had advanced just two months during grades three to five of public school.

I felt frustrated and angry—at the teachers and at the system. I thought of the kids who never would have the chance to learn what we were able to give Paul. He had worked at the mechanics of reading but never really understood that the purpose of reading was to convey information or thoughts from the author to the reader. He's an intelligent kid and was never a behavior problem in school but somehow he had become invisible in the classrooms of thirty kids. No teacher had ever taken a personal interest in him. I have wondered since how many other invisible kids are institutionalized out there by the state, whose parents were unaware or possibly didn't even care. I just had to remedy that for Paul.

I made him read out loud and then we would discuss what he had read. He didn't like reading aloud and wasn't too good at it, but read aloud he did. And he also began to learn what the words were saying to *him*. In a few months he reached the sixth grade reading level, and we were able to concentrate on other areas.

We mingled the self-learn method of our home school with other meaningful activities. Meanwhile, Paul continued in Boy Scouts and spent "school time" working toward being an Eagle

Scout. He was hardly in a social straightjacket as many suppose about home schoolers. He took the American Red Cross first-aid and disaster-training classes and worked with the Red Cross all during Hurricane David. Now, that was some education! He learned CPR (cardio-pulmonary resuscitation) and gave 175 CPR demonstrations in one day to a curious public. The American Red Cross wanted to use him for an instructor, and he would have been delighted except that the ARC manual required that he be sixteen first.

Once Paul had caught up and was ahead of his agemates, he went back to a private church school for a couple of years, but our finances forced him into home school again. He had enjoyed the private school but was also contented at home. His teacher from the church school worked very closely with me. We appreciated that dear lady.

The family is the basic unit of a continuing society and we found that home school strengthened our family unit. Most parents see their kids hardly more than an hour or so a day. Many, we were told, especially fathers, don't see them that much a week. Children spend more time with peers than with their families and the pressure to conform is so great that even the strongest child is usually affected. We learned that this leads to peer dependency, a social cancer that eats out self-worth and robs the child of moral values and ability to make sound decisions.

We study together, work together, play together. The kids invite us into many of their extra-curricular activities. We have grown stronger together.

I would be less than honest to leave the impression that it has always been easy. Anyone who claims that teaching their kids at home is always a bed of roses is dishonest, naive or a very rare saint. Children are not always self-motivating, and there have been some heavy days! But, like childbirth, it's well worth the effort. The pain is quickly forgotten.

Paul will soon graduate—early—from high school. He studies three hours a day. That is sufficient when studying alone. And he has a part-time job selling shoes and sporting goods in a local department store.

Sometimes I ponder on the problems we had trying to establish our home school and on the questions and accusations hurled our way. Fortunately, only a few said "smother mother," or threatened "social misfit," but I wish all could be around to see the finished product: Paul bending over "Annie" demonstrating CPR, or smiling at the results of his achievement tests or selling to a customer at the department store. I really think they would smile, too. We wouldn't take anything in the world for our experience with home school.

TWELVE

We Single Girls

Last night as we (Raymond and Dorothy Moore) were editing the earlier chapters of this book, we received a telephone call from Jeanne Dempsey, who lives in a small town in northeastern Washington. Her husband, Allen, is a lumberjack and she is a high-school-educated mother with two children, eleven and ten. Jeanne is a quiet but articulate person who has very high expectations for her two boys. She and her husband have deep religious convictions and are convinced that the public schools of her area, five miles away, do not offer an education consistent with their family values. But the nearest church school is twenty-five miles away and that is too far for such tender spirits to negotiate.

So the Dempseys took their children out of school to educate them at home and arranged for an effective course of study which was compatible with their beliefs. But the trouble is, that particular course is not known in Washington state, so is not officially accredited.

"So," warned a local school official, "you must put your child back into school or *we will take your children away from you.*"

So wastes the most cruel of all crimes of the State in our

121

democracy. And at the heart of this crime is the astonishing failure of public officials to distinguish between those parents who have a deep concern for their children and other parents who couldn't care less. They are like physicians who can't tell the difference between a person who is well and one who is sick. The laws, if they are worth the paper they are written on, are made to protect children from parents who don't care. But to move away from the intent of these laws and to apply them to parents who are deeply committed to the welfare of their children, is in itself a criminal miscarriage of justice.

Such officials should be pursued court, not only by injunction, but by class action suits which address the most fundamental issues of constitutional law—in this case, the guarantee of the First Amendment of the Constitution as repeatedly interpreted by the U.S. Supreme Court: Parents have the prior right to determine the education of their children as long as they maintain academic achievement records and behavior standards which are compatible with state standards.

Jeanne Dempsey is married to a strong-minded man who gives her a great deal of comfort in perplexity. But there are some parents who do not have such support. These single parents, usually mothers, are nevertheless faced sometimes with the very same threats—in their cases, more cruel than ever. We usually say "mothers" because although there is occasionally a single father who teaches his children at home, men do not tend to remain single as long as women who have children they must carry into a new marriage.

So we tell you here the brief stories of four great women who had the courage and insight and sheer mothering power to face up to charges which in some cases labeled them as criminals. We will take them from four points of the compass: Patty Blankenship of Atlanta, Barbara Franz of New York, Judy Waddell in Berrien Springs, Michigan, and Vickie Singer of Kamas, Utah. And we will close with the very special story of Vickie Singer, a martyr's widow.

PATTY BLANKENSHIP

One day while we were doing an interview on WRNG, Atlanta's "Ring Radio," a light feminine voice came urgently over the telephone. After the show, we were told that she had called later and requested to meet us at the station. It was Patty Blankenship, a single mother of two young sons, Mark (eleven) and Patrick (eight). The Dekalb County Juvenile Court were threatening to take her children from her, to fine her a thousand dollars a day and to put her in jail—remarkable retribution for being a good mother.

In 1974, five years earlier, Patrick's kindergarten teacher thought that he was too young and immature to be in school, so Patty brought him home. This alerted her to the importance of readiness for schooling. He did so well at home that she decided to keep him out another year. It was then, in 1975, that the authorities went after her, threatening jail, heavy fines and, worst of all, to take her boys away from her.

This discouraging situation was further complicated by an infection in Patrick's leg which became so serious the surgeons advised amputation. Patty said she would stay home and personally nurse the child before she would permit him to lose his leg. And this she did, sewing for a living, occasionally modeling shoes, and doing anything else on a part-time basis in which she could pick up a few dollars to support her little family and avoid the onus of welfare lines.

She used materials from the Christian Liberty Academy (see Appendix A) and worked to keep her boys well above average in their schoolwork and distinctly superior to most children in their behavior.

A few well-meaning friends joined school officials in pointing out the social "losses" the boys would "suffer" by missing school. Patty not only pointed out that she was keeping Mark home with Patrick to give him company, but also that Patrick was now admired by the Atlanta Flames hockey team; theirs was hardly a case of social deprivation. Nevertheless, school officials continued to harass Patty and her two young sons.

Meanwhile, Patty began studying up on child development and school law, including her constitutional rights. We found when we talked with her in August of 1979 that she had already read our books and articles on early schooling and child development. She became enough of an expert on constitutional law that she knew more than the officials who were challenging her. This in part accounts for her managing to delay a formal trial from 1975 to early 1980. During this period, she had brought both of the boys a grade or two above average for their ages, and had managed in the process to save Patrick's leg—except for surgery now planned to lengthen it.

In September, 1979 Attorney Michael Parham of Atlanta— also a Baptist minister—wrote asking for preliminary information. Five months later he wrote again on behalf also of Attorney Ted Price and Patty Blankenship, requesting that we witness at her trial. All counsels and witnesses concerned agreed to donate their time in view of Patty's financial hardship. All concerned believed in view of the attitude voiced by the Dekalb County Juvenile Court that a jury trial should be requested.

This decision turned out to be sound, for the judge appointed turned out to be one who was reputed to work hand-in-glove with the prosecutor with whom he was often teamed. It was difficult for the defense to ask a question without the prosecutor shouting, "I object!" Almost inevitably, and it seemed, automatically, the judge would mutter "Sustained." The court record will bear this out.

And of course, in questioning, the prosecutor would shout at us that he wanted only yes or no answers. After a series of standoffs, we were constrained to advise him that we had raised our hand to tell the truth, and that unless he phrased his questions appropriately, he would receive a definitive answer or no answer at all. This legal charade and a sound defense case had its effect on the jury, and Patty was acquitted. Today, she continues to teach her children at home, and is so thoroughly acquainted with state and national law that she is considering running for public office. She is already conducting seminars for lawyers. And . . . with her new qualifications as a home-school specialist, she has become regional representative for a home-school publisher.

BARBARA FRANZ

Barbara Franz, a Queens, New York, widow, was working hard to rear her three children, Susan, Peter and John. Both Susan and Peter had already been in school for some time, and she duly enrolled John when he was turning six. But before long she observed that he was becoming churlish, generally fretful and so hyperactive that he was unable to concentrate on anything for more than a few seconds. She volunteered as a teacher's aide at Johnny's public school classroom and was gladly accepted. But before long she realized that her boy had no business in this room. The academic climate seemed about average as New York City primary schools go, but she was certain that the emotional and moral environment was not what she wanted for her youngest son, and she took him out of school.

The little blond, mop-haired youngster was delighted, and the churlishness, fretfulness and hyperactivity of the six year old seemed now to be transferred to the officials of Public School 207. Barbara was haled into Queens Family Court.

The Honorable Saul Moskoff, judge of the family court in Jamaica, New York, listened patiently. He seemed well aware of Barbara's fine qualifications as a mother and as a teacher. He listened intently both to witnesses for the prosecution and those of us who witnessed for the defense.

Defense lawyer Steven Schwartz pointed out first that even though Barbara Franz had technically violated section 1012 of the Family Court Act, she was not really in violation of the intention of the legislature—which was concerned that children not be neglected. It was clear that her home environment was "superior" to that of the public schools. Second, the defense observed that Mrs. Franz "through the use of superior teaching methods," had not only satisfied but had surpassed New York education law Article 65, Section 3204 (2) and its requirement that a substantially equivalent education be given to children who attend school elsewhere than at a public school.

Third, he protested that Section 3201 (2) of education law arbitrarily required home tutoring for at least as many hours as public school instruction. Anyone who has had experience in home schooling or understands the educational process—the difference between individual tutoring and teaching in a class of twenty or thirty children—knows that you can accomplish as much in an hour and a half or so with one child as a teacher of twenty or thirty children can during the whole school day.

Fourth, Attorney Schwartz insisted that the New York compulsory education law directly impinges upon the fundamental guarantee of privacy and must therefore be set aside as unconstitutional. New York officials did not understand this so well back in 1975 and 1976 during this case, as they do today. In 1980, New York State educational officials became more compassionate toward home schooling, as it became apparent that such parents generally did a superior job of teaching.

Fifth, and finally, Schwartz pointed out that the "compulsory education law of New York has failed to achieve its objectives" and therefore he insisted that it was not responsive to the purposes and intentions of the legislature and should be set aside. This has not yet been done legally, but has been set aside in practice. After the trial was over, Judge Moskoff called me into his chambers apologetically. He was a gentle and kindly Jewish man who had been thoughtful of Barbara and the children throughout the whole scene. He expressed generous appreciation of my witness, and said he agreed.

"But," he pointed out to me, "the New York law is very specific, and I have no recourse but to find Mrs. Franz in violation of these attendance laws."

Barbara Franz, by continued appeals, managed to keep her

young son out for another year or two, until he was reasonably ready to go to school. Our last report is that in his studies and attitudes, he is doing very well indeed.

In this case the judge felt bound by the letter of the law more than by the needs of the child. Fortunately, this is seldom true throughout the courts of this nation. Nevertheless, it should alert us all to the importance of giving closer attention to legislation that affects our children. For when our Hewitt public policy research team at Stanford studied the fifty states of the U.S., we could not find one early-schooling attendance law that was based upon systematic, replicable research. Some of the laws came into force almost by accident and some were surest comedies of error.

JUDY WADDELL

In late 1974, Judy Waddell received a letter from the Berrien Springs Superintendent of Schools stating that Bret must be enrolled in school by the given date, a few days away.

She had deliberately kept Bret, now seven, out of school—in Michigan, a state which requires little children to be in school by age six. According to his pediatrician, Bret's physical growth was about two years behind the average seven-year-old's. A psychologist had observed that Bret's psychological and emotional maturation levels were quite uneven. This may have been due to an inherited developmental pattern and/or influenced by the family breakup. Some time before, Judy's husband (Bret's father) had chosen to give up his Christian convictions and find companionship which would accommodate that choice. Whatever the cause, both the pediatrician and one psychologist intimated to Judy that Bret was not really ready for school.

Although Mrs. Waddell had only a high school education and a stenographic course at a business college, she read avidly anything and everything worthwhile about children. She had read, among other things, that most children could benefit by a delay in school entry. She had learned the importance of spending a great deal of time with her young son, of reading to him daily and having many good books available for him to "read." She often took him with her in her many efforts to help her neighbors. While Judy accepted state aid so that she could be home with Bret during his preschool years, she also helped to support herself with part-time secretarial work and babysitting in her home. She felt that state aid is given in order for mothers to care for their children, so they can spend both quality and quantity time with them.

But now there was word that there could be problems if he were not enrolled in school. While she quietly waited, she checked to see what could be done to cooperate and yet do what was best for Bret. At one point someone suggested that Bret could be taken away from her. Finally, she was threatened with a fine or jail sentence. Without the normal strength and consolation of a husband, some expected Judy Waddell to panic. But Judy, a woman of prayer, seemed to become stronger, until one day the sheriff's squad car drove up in front of her house and two big, hulking, but sheepish officers apologetically led her to the car and drove her to the St. Joseph County jail. She was booked on a charge of criminal misdemeanor (child neglect). She was photographed, just like any other criminal, relieved of her few valuables, and placed in the "holding tank" in the inner jail.

It was at that time that my secretary called long distance and advised me of these events. An attorney was obtained by her church which she contacted via a call from the police station.

An interesting commentary in Judy's case is that the local school district made no effort whatsoever to examine her child physically or psychologically or academically. And the school headquarters at a higher level which governs attendance over several Michigan districts did no detailed inquiry or study whatsoever. Both the school superintendent and the regional attendance officer operated strictly in terms of the letter of the law without any reference whatsoever to the needs of the child. In fairness to public schools, we add that this is not standard practice.

When Mrs. Waddell was brought into court for a pretrial hearing, Judge John Hammond was astonished that she would even challenge this attendance law. He set a date for the trial and suggested that it should be over in a matter of "several hours," but Judge Hammond did not know much of the lady that he had on his hands and her determination to give her child the best of a mother's care. With the help of a number of friends and of her church, expert witnesses were brought in from coast to coast, and the trial continued for most of a year—a mixture of an overloaded court and a great deal of unnecessary testimony. That trial, which began October 2, 1975, still had not been resolved as of the writing of this book in early 1982.

Judy Waddell kept Bret out of school until he was eight years of age—then she enrolled him in a half-day kindergarten in order to have "peace." She would have preferred to have kept him home one or two years longer, then started him in second or third grade, for which she would have prepared him academically. When the little boy enrolled in school at age eight, his math tested at grade 2.6, and his vocabulary skills tested at grade 4.4, without an hour of formal instruction in all of his young life. Judy Waddell is now a certified Iowa teacher and her young son is an outstanding student in achievement and behavior. He is an early fourteen, and high in the eighth grade.

VICKIE SINGER

The story of John and Vickie Singer of Kamas, Utah, is quite well known across the nation. We were called in to counsel with the Singers shortly after their three oldest children had been evaluated by the State. Reporters told us that they had been declared by the state-appointed psychometrist to be "asocial, of ghetto mentality and brain damaged." The most shameful part of this was that the psychologist had so reported the Singer children—Heidi (thirteen), Suzanne (twelve) and Tim (eleven)—in an interview over national television.

Against this background, one must understand that John Singer came out of the World War II Holocaust. He was a part-Jewish German who had been converted to Mormonism and a man of very deep convictions. In the course of some changes in the doctrine or practice of the Mormon church, he came into disagreement with the hierarchy and was excommunicated. This put him out of favor with the run-of-the-mill Mormon in his community and endeared him to other Mormons who also had doctrinal problems.

Meanwhile, John's convictions brought him other perplexities. He was distressed at "error that was being taught as truth" in the schools his children were attending, and decided to take them out and to teach them at home. He went so far as to build a special little schoolhouse for the Singer school, a few yards away from their home on the two-and-a-half acre pad on the side of the mountain above Kamas.

The schoolroom was equipped sparsely but adequately with blackboards, a number of "decent" books, a variety of school helps, and—in that cold area—a good woodburning stove. School time, taught mostly by the father and a little by the mother, was augmented with many other activities. All of the children learned how to clean house and to cook and sew and do the laundry. Each of them could bake a good loaf of bread.

That was remarkable enough in this age. But John and Vickie Singer sensed that their oldest daughter, Heidi, had vocal talent, so they arranged to give her professional singing lessons in a town close to the home. Suzanne, their second daughter, obviously had an artistic bent, so they gave her professional art lessons in the big town. And she has sold a number of her paintings—generally of much better quality than the average college art student.

Tim's speciality was building log cabins. He was not satisfied with the first one, so built a second. He did it all by himself except with a little help from his father in establishing the cut and angle on his rafters—a difficult enough chore for most carpenters. His genius was so remarkable that in his eleventh and twelfth years he built two go-carts, totally out of scraps, scrounged from wherever he could find them, complete with wheels, brakes, gears, drive chains, clutches and all the power and comforts of a first-class little-man's machine. He was not satisfied with the first vehicle so he made the second—something that few mature men can do. And he did this *after* his father died.

These were the children who, upon the protest of a few neighbors and the State, were forced to submit to an evaluation by the state psychometrist, who himself had nine children, yet who admitted to me that he had not "looked into the character" of the Singer children. Even without arguing their brilliance, this trio was the most remarkable to me for their near-perfect social poise. On each of my visits to their humble home, I was treated in a genteel and well-mannered, but enthusiastic way. And all of their letters to me meanwhile had been carefully punctuated and neatly written in excellent, well-expressed English. These are the children who the state allegedly charged were suffering from criminal neglect.

Meanwhile, John had ingratiated himself with the local public school superintendent by rescuing his son from drowning. But that was not enough to save him from persecution of a determined state and a hostile neighborhood.

Then came the national news media report of the state psychometrist's evaluations, referred to earlier, that the children were asocial, of ghetto mentality and . . . brain damaged. John and his wife were upset by this, yet that is not the primary reason John refused to let anyone else test his children. He and Vickie believed that God had given them children with the command to be guardians and overseers of them. They did not want to give up this happy duty to the state. To allow the state to test and train them, the Singers felt, was a denial of their religious freedom and God-given task to train their children themselves.

"I would rather die than give myself into the hands of the law," John declared. "I cannot compromise these precious things and live with myself."

Some of us worked with John and Vickie Singer while authorities were trying to trick them one way or another into custody—pretending at one time to be *Los Angeles Times* reporters.

John was not an aggressive, violent man, but a man of peace. He took as his motto, "Stand your ground—don't fire unless fired upon." As it turned out a week or so later, in his last moments of life, he chose to turn and leave those who were pursuing him. In the presence of some of his children, he received nine fatal shots in his back. Many say that this cannot happen in America today. An important court case will soon reveal just how much it can, for the Singer case is being prepared as this book goes to press.

We tell this story near the end of this book to demonstrate how important to some people children can be, and how indifferent to a child's welfare the State and unthinking neighbors can become.

Meanwhile, Vickie continues to teach her children at home. After visiting her recently, and reading the children's letters, we judge they are doing well indeed. Vickie no longer is hearing the State protest, but she is also no longer hearing the strong supporting words of her husband, John. A very strong woman, Vickie Singer, as the behavior of her children evidences in the face of some neighbors who still do not understand. By hard work and frugality she manages to eke out a living for her brood.

John Singer's rigidity—or his peculiar beliefs—cost him his life, but coming out of the Holocaust as he did, we are not particularly surprised at his actions. He lived his life by his principles and he did not surrender principle easily. Perhaps we can stand a few more principled parents. Indeed, if we do not have a lot more of them soon, we will shortly lose America as we now know her.

THIRTEEN

How to Deal with the Law

When you proceed in a businesslike manner in dealing step by step with the legal issues, you seldom have to go to court. And it is worth your effort to avoid such a confrontation if you can do it without violating principle. The United States Supreme Court held in the *Wisconsin v. Yoder* case (Amish) that school officials must apply a three-pronged test whenever faced with religiously based requests for exemption from attendance laws.

First, you must have a *firm* religious or philosophical *conviction.* Your right to the exercise of this freedom is protected by the First Amendment of the Constitution. But it must be a sincerely held belief. If there is any reasonable hope that you will eventually "cave in" or if you enroll your child in a public or private school "while you get the situation settled," the school officials will sense your lack of conviction and often will continue to threaten, harass, or intimidate you. They may keep after you until you do give up or they can show in court that you have only a preference and not a conviction. Religion in the view of the Supreme Court does not require membership in any particular denomination or sect.

Second, you must know why you want to operate a home school. The reasons should be expressed in positive terms, such as: "We feel it is our duty and obligation to be the teacher of,

133

and models for, the social and character values of our children,"
"Our children will grow up so quickly we feel it our right and
privilege to enjoy their companionship in these early years," or
"We believe on the basis of experience and research that a quiet,
cooperative, and family-oriented environment is conducive to
the best academic learning and social development." This helps
to answer the second prong of the Yoder case, namely, "Does the
application of the compulsory school attendance law infringe on
the right of free exercise of religion?"

Third, you must have a written plan of procedure or schedule,
you must be prepared to show the materials you use, and you
must give other proof that the children are being educated, not
neglected. * This means that neighbors should not be seeing
children running around unsupervised most or much of the day.
Neither should they have reason to suspect that children are
being left at home alone or that television is the main teacher
and baby-sitter. You need this evidence to pass the third prong—
"Does the state have an interest of sufficient magnitude to over-
ride the claim of violation of the right to free exercise of religion?" Remember, judges are impressed by well-kept diaries.

Then the burden of proof falls on the state to prove that you
are not providing good education for your child. To require that
a child must be educated to become a productive citizen is in fact
the state's right and obligation.

Since each state is different, study your state laws well, including home-school or private-school provisions. In many states
there is no compulsion for children to attend any kind of school
until age seven or even eight. Some parents assume that because
most children enter at age five, the state requires it. This is
seldom, if ever, true. If home education is not mentioned in the
state code, incorporating as a private school is an excellent way.
The cost is usually $50.00 or less if you do it yourself through one
of the offices of your Secretary of State.

When you have learned who has the administrative responsi-

---

*See also the authors' Home Grown Kids and their Better Late Than Early for
programs.

bility to enforce your law, you may have to do some research to find out the best approach. Discreet inquiries of state school officials and local people are usually helpful. Try to get in touch with a local or state home-schooling support group which keeps in touch with local and state issues.* Then you will know whether or not you have reasonable people with whom to deal and what precedents have been set. Remember, school officials have difficulty being objective when enrollment is dropping and state dollars are lost. Often they are less informed about the law than you.

Some are even suspected of making up their own "laws." For example, we were called by a parent in Pennsylvania who had taken her child out of first grade at age seven and was teaching her at home. The social worker sent this woman a form letter threatening a fine or imprisonment if the child was not back in school in five days. Of course, the mother was panic-stricken, so we volunteered to call the officials. The principal of the school explained that even though the maximum entry age for schooling in Pennsylvania was not until eight years, a child who had previously enrolled could not be withdrawn. When we asked for the source of that regulation, he referred us to the school attorney, who in turn assured us that the principal was mistaken and agreed to inform him. He added that, coincidentally, he was just about to leave the office to speak to a group of school officials regarding the state school laws because, he confided, they were not well informed.

If you find your superintendent to be resistant or threatening, let him know kindly and firmly that you have not come to this decision lightly and are prepared to go to court. You may even advise him, or utilize someone authoritative to tell him or other concerned judges, prosecutors, state officials, etc., what has been happening in similar court cases around the nation. Decisions have overwhelmingly favored parents, and most have

---

*You may send a self-addressed, *stamped* envelope to the Hewitt Research Foundation, 36211 S.E. Sunset View, Washougal, WA 98671, for names and addresses of support groups.

proved an embarrassment not only to the school district but to the school officials themselves. Seldom will any school district that has had this experience repeat it. Such careful preventive action avoids court summons in at least nine out of ten cases.

But far more important than the success of parents in court are the needs of young children. Few teachers or administrators are taught adequately about how children develop and learn. It is of utmost important that no one be allowed to abuse or reject our children—which is exactly what is happening when they are institutionalized too early.

If the unlikely time does come when you are called to court for either a preliminary hearing or an actual trial, make sure that you have done your homework. Most district attorneys, judges, and educators know very little about home schools and how well they perform. They know remarkably little about parents' rights and how they are assured by the Constitution as interpreted by the U.S. Supreme Court in a series of decisions over the last sixty years. And some know astonishingly little about the winning history of other home school cases even—as happened in Nebraska—if they were only a few miles down the road and had been affirmed by the state supreme court.

Now is your time to do some teaching to these public servants, but don't attempt to teach unless you know what you are teaching. This is what this chapter is all about.

In the first place you will be greatly helped if you carefully reread the earlier chapters of this book and all of *Home Grown Kids.* Also *Better Late Than Early* ** will tell you how normal children develop and why they should not be in school before ages eight or ten. Included in the discussion are sound research-bases for all conclusions. Obtain a copy of your own state school laws and local statutes, if any—as they relate to home schools. Study them carefully. Follow with a careful scrutiny of all avail-

*Waco, TX: Word Books, Publisher, 1981.
**A Reader's Digest book available through Hewitt Research Foundation, 36211 S.E. Sunset View, Washougal, WA 98671.

able cases that may have any relationship to your particular problem. See, for example, the appendices of this book.

Following this chapter are several appendices involving home-school cases as they were actually presented in or stated by the courts. We have not included complete cases, for this would take many books. But we do provide conclusions or briefs from several trials and pretrial hearings to illustrate key points in preparing your defense. For example:

1. *Larry W. and Judy B. O'Guin:* A petition by the prosecuting attorney and the district judge which points out that the district court in Marquette, Michigan, was not in their opinion the place to deal with a home-school problem. In other words, this case was refused in court, as is true in most cases.

2. *Larry and Nell Williams:* Another case strongly stressing religious convictions in which the district attorney threw the case out of court because it lacked "strong proof that a child's failure to attend school until he has reached a sufficient maturity, that is, somewhere between the ages of eight and ten," would make him a burden to the state. Note that the prosecutor concluded that even if he obtained a conviction at the trial level, he would probably lose it on appeal.

3. *Leslie and Vicki Rice:* The findings in a Nebraska case which was won by the Rices in the district court but was appealed by the prosecutor to the state supreme court. That court upheld the Rices' victory at the district level.

4. *Kenneth and Bonnie Wenberg:* A summary of the defense attorney's appeal on behalf of a couple who, after they had won their case in juvenile court found that the *ad litem* attorney whom the court assigned as guardian to young Erik Wenberg during the trial, was now appealing the judge's decision. This is a summation of the defense attorney's successful brief before the higher court.

5. *Patty Blankenship:* One of the most complete pretrial briefs we have seen—presented by attorneys. This one was prepared for the trial of a single mother who won in an Atlanta, Georgia, trial. This case was tried before a judge and prosecutor whom, we

were warned in advance, worked "hand-in-glove"—the judge nearly always sustaining the prosecutor's objections to the defense's line of questioning. So the defense asked for a jury trial and was rewarded with an acquittal.

These findings and briefs are not offered to take the place of competent legal counsel. You should make every effort to insure that you have an attorney who is not only capable, but who is sympathetic to the home-school ideal. Many lawyers are afraid to take such cases for fear that they will convey the impression that they are against the public schools, and therefore place their reputations in jeopardy in their communities. Yet there is a growing list of attorneys, nationwide, who are becoming familiar with family school problems and are skillful at handling them in court. A list of their names, along with a kit of other up-to-date information, may be obtained by sending a self-addressed double-stamped envelope with a check for ten dollars to the Hewitt Research Foundation, 36211 S.E. Sunset View, Washougal, WA 98671.

Acting as your own attorney. We do *not* recommend that you act as your own attorney unless it is absolutely necessary. If it is in fact impossible for you to afford an attorney, and if a court-appointed attorney is not assigned to you, be sure you closely study other cases before presenting your own in court. If it is absolutely necessary for you to act as your own attorney, write to the Hewitt address above for materials of cases in which parents have defended themselves. We suggest a donation of at least five dollars to help defray costs and a self-addressed stamped envelope. We are working hard to develop a legal assistance network to avoid such lay involvement in defense.

Attorney costs. Many parents fear the costs involved in defending such a case. Investigate as carefully as you can the availability of attorneys who might handle your case, and frankly ask them their estimated costs. Some attorneys who are usually sympathetic to such cases and who are inclined to be altruistic, may give you a very reasonable estimate. But ask for the estimate in writing. A few other generous lawyers who strongly favor the place of the home school in our educational system sometimes will make no charge at all, or charge only for the costs of travel. You should make every effort in such cases to accommodate these individuals in the same thoughtful spirit they treat you.

Civil Rights. There is a time when parents may retrieve their attorneys' fees by suing their accusers. As this right becomes better known, schools, child protective services and other agencies of the state may think twice before prosecuting worthy parents. And even the teacher unions and other vested interests would be wise to be more cautious.

Under provisions of sections 1983, 1985, 1986 and 1988 of Chapter 42 the U.S. Civil Rights Act, parents are given remarkable recourse when harassed by public officials. For example, many parents submit to questioning, testing, and continual other demands without sound reason. Often this amounts to genuine harassment. Frequently parents are well within the local and state laws as well as the constitutional rights they are claiming. In one New Jersey case, a young mother was repeatedly accused by the school superintendent. The sympathetic judge threw the case out of court. But the frustrated schoolman took the mother to another court on another charge. He got the child protective services, health department, and even the fire department and attorney general involved in the act. Such a case invites suit for harassment.

Section 1983 provides for "deprivation of rights"; 1985 deals with "conspiracy to interfere," and 1988 allows for payment of attorneys' fees by the harassing agency. Section 1986 makes vulnerable even those public agencies, teachers, unions or others that could have intervened on behalf of the parent, but failed to do so. These sections are included in Appendix G of this book. If you sense harassment, get reputable legal advice to see if these sections relate to you.

Your witnesses. You may have a variety of witnesses, including neighbors, pastor, and friends, but expert professional witnesses are particularly crucial—at least as important as having a good attorney, and in some cases much more so. Wherever possible, select as witnesses those with successful court experience who are well acquainted with research facts related to home schooling, who understand how young children learn, and who are intimately acquainted with the school scene. A good witness will supply common sense as well as a knowledge of education. He or she will clearly show the relationship of the home to the school and will document the general superiority of home schools— including their record as the world's greatest producer of leadership and genius (see chapter 1) and the likelihood that children educated in them will have little delinquency and will become social leaders (see chapter 12).

The books *Home-Grown Kids* and *Home-Spun Schools*, with our coming "Mystery Kids" series will likely help you, but also, when placed in the hands of educators who might have become antagonists, they may also bring understanding. Show local educators the books and ask them if they have any evidence to contradict what those books say. If you are called into court, make sure that the books are placed in the hands of your chief witnesses, for many otherwise capable psychologists and educators do not have this information. And be certain that your lawyers have read these books. For sound research evidence read *Better Late Than Early* (for parents) or *School Can Wait* (for professionals), both available from Hewitt Research.

The accompanying table lists states and their attitudes toward home schools. This information was compiled from studies by Charles Marston of the New Hampshire State Department of Education, 1980; Patricia Lines of the Education Commission of the States, 1982; and The Hewitt Research Foundation, 1975, 1982. Bear in mind that state laws and policies may be capricious, changing from one stance to another over short periods, depending on the whims and pressures of legislators and citizens.

Some states may say "yes" to home schools but educators may not know. In Missouri recently, several home-schooling parents were threatened but were quickly vindicated when the state attendance chief was notified and information was sent out to

SCHOOL ENTRANCE AGES AND HOME SCHOOL PERMISSIONS

State	Entrance Age	Permission	Code or Statute Section
Alabama	7	Yes[3,4]	16–28–5 (1975)
Alaska	7	Yes	14.30.010(b)(10 & 11)(1981)
Arizona	8	Yes	15–802(B)(1)(Supp. 1981)
Arkansas	7	No[1]	1502 (1980)
California	6	Yes	48224 (Wests 1978)
Colorado	7	Yes	22–33–104(2)(i)(1973)
Connecticut	7	Yes	10–184 (1981)
Delaware	6	Yes	tit. 14, Sec. 2703 (1981)
Dist. of Col.	7	Yes	31–401 (1981)
Florida	6	Yes[4]	232.02(4)(1977); Op. Atty. Gen. 072–90, 3/22/72
Georgia	7	No[1]	32–21 (1980, Amended by Supp. 1981)
Hawaii	6	Yes	298–9(2)(1976); 298–9(6)(Supp. 1981)
Idaho	7	Yes	33–202 (1981)
Illinois	7	Yes[2]	Ch. 122, sec. 26–1 (Supp. 1981–1982)
Indiana	7	Yes[3]	20–8.1–3–1 et seq. (Cum. Supp. 1981)
Iowa	7	Yes[4]	299.1 & 4 (1981)
Kansas	7	No[1]	72–1111(d) (1981)
Kentucky	6	No[1,3]	159.010 (Bobbs Merrill 1980)
Louisiana	7	Yes	17:236 (West Supp. 1981)
Maine	7	Yes	tit. 20, Sec. 911(3)(a) (Supp. 1981–1982)
Maryland	6	Yes	7–301 (1978)
Massachu- setts	varies	Yes[2]	ch. 76, Sec. 1 (West Supp. 1981)

(continued)

141

State	Entrance Age	Permission	Code or Statute Section
Michigan	6	Yes[4]	A. G. Op. No. 5579, Sept. 27, 1979
Minnesota	7	No[1,3]	120.10 (West Cum. Supp. 1981)
Mississippi	7	Yes	37–13–97 (1981 Cum. Supp.)
Missouri	7	Yes	167.031 (Supp. 1982)
Montana	7	Yes	20–5–102 (2)(c); 20–10–121(3–4); 20–7–116(1981)
Nebraska	7	No[1,2]	79–201 (1976)
Nevada	7	Yes	392–070 (1979)
New Hampshire	7	Yes	193.1 (1977)
New Jersey	6	Yes[2]	18a; 38–25 (West 1968)
New Mexico	6	Yes	22–12–2 (Supp. 1981)
New York	6	Yes	3204.2 (McKinney 1981)
North Carolina	7	No[5]	115C–378 (Cum. Supp. 1981)
North Dakota	7	No[4]	15–34.1–01 (1981)
Ohio	6	Yes[3]	3321.04(A)(2) (Page's 1980)
Oklahoma	7	No[1,5]	tit. 70, sec. 10–105 (West Cum. Supp. 1981)
Oregon	7	Yes	339.030(6) (1979)

State			
Pennsylvania	8	Yes	tit. 24, sec. 13–1327 (Purdon Supp. 1981)
Puerto Rico	8	No	tit. 29, sec. 450 (1966)
Rhode Island	7	Yes[4]	16–19–1 (1981)
South Carolina	7	Yes	59–65–10 (Cum. Supp. 1931)
South Dakota	7	Yes	Comp. Laws. Ann. 13–27–3 (1975)
Tennessee	7	No[1]	49–1708 & 49–1710 (Bobbs Merrill 1977)
Texas	7	No[1]	tit. 2, sec. 21.032 (Vernon Supp. 1981)
Utah	6	Yes	53–24–1(b)(2) (1970)
Vermont	7	Yes	tit. 16, sec. 1121(b) (1974)
Virginia	5	Yes	22.1–254 (1980)
Washington	8	Yes[4]	28A.27.010 (Cum. Supp. 1981)
West Virginia	7	Yes	18–8–1 (1977)
Wisconsin	6	No[3,4]	118.15(4) (Supp. 1981–1982)
Wyoming	7	No[5]	21–4–102(a)(iii) (1977)

[1]Some home schools operate by incorporating as a private school.
[2]Permitted as a result of court cases.
[3]May be exempted for religious or conscientious reasons.
[4]Requires certified teacher, only part time in some cases.
[5]Other exemptions may be available.

school districts. Other states that say "yes" may, like Colorado, have their caveats. In Colorado the present state school administration is friendly in giving approval authorized by law, but the next one may not be so generous. Still others, like Montana, say "yes" but limit permissions to students who live more than an hour away or who are handicapped. Most of the "yeses" have limitations of some kind.

And some may say "no" when in fact the states are quite large-hearted. California law says "no," yet in most cases approval is contingent only upon filing an affidavit with the county school superintendent. The main exception is the Los Angeles City and County, whose officials, under pressure to maintain teacher jobs, are still asserting their "higher" requirements (even though many of their public schools are among the worst in the state and their home schools among the best). And in still other "no" states like Georgia and Nebraska and Illinois, the courts have upheld conscientious parents.

Ask your state school official for copies of appropriate sections of school laws. The table provided here includes up-to-date sources as of middle-1982. If parents and teachers who want home schools work closely with legislators, this picture could change favorably soon. This would be an excellent way to make these pages out of date.

We find that only about ten home schools out of a hundred are threatened with court action. And in eight or nine cases out of the ten where they are challenged, tactful handling of educators, prosecutors and judges will probably quiet the issue. And the parents may never be brought to court. But in those few cases that are litigated—whether for preliminary hearing or actual trial—the Boy Scouts' motto is appropriate: "Be prepared." So we offer you in the next few pages the selection of materials mentioned in this chapter with the hope that you will read them as if your case depended upon it, for indeed it may. They will also give you some encouraging insights on how other brave parents have gone on before you to help smooth your way.

Appendix A

HOME-SCHOOL RESOURCES
and Supplemental School Materials

If you are beginning a home school, it is usually best to use a home instruction course, at least for the first year or two. We recommend the kind that (1) contains carefully selected Christ-centered materials from a variety of publishing houses; (2) is not too structured (heavily workbook-oriented); (3) avoids myths and nonsense stories; (4) plans for no formal schooling before about eight or ten, then starting the child with his or her agemates; (5) lists costs clearly and specifies what services are offered (personal counsel, tests, legal advice, etc.); (6) includes clear instructions for students and teacher; (7) encourages discussion, creativity, and independent thought; and (8) gives counsel in dealing with the law.

Since we published a general list of quite good schools in our book *Home-Grown Kids*, parents and other educators have underscored these criteria. Some outstanding Southern Baptists, for example, expressed disappointment that we would recommend an organization which used the McGuffey readers. We wondered why, because historians suggest that America reached her highest level of literacy—over 99 percent—during the early McGuffey period. We were not aware at the time that the books widely sold for the last 100 years as McGuffeys were really not the original, God-centered books written by W. H. McGuffey, but were only patterned after the McGuffey readers. One McGuffey specialist advised us that they were more humanistically edited to please public school people who wanted less of God in the curriculum.

The original W. H. McGuffey books were written and revised in the 1830s and 1840s. Mr. McGuffey's brother, Alexander, picked up where W. H. left off, writing and revising into the 1860s. But the "public school McGuffeys" were not published until around 1879. Many are nevertheless pleased with them because "They are much better than most books around today," and, indeed they are. Furthermore, they did not omit God altogether. Some even call them "Christian McGuffeys." Yet others consider them a fraud because "they are not what they pretended to be—real McGuffeys," and because they "have more mythical material than God."

Recently, for these and other reasons, we have been asked by some publishers to "prepare for publication" the original four readers. This requires updating in spelling, punctuation and word usage. It also will eliminate an outdated story on whale-killing which offends many parents and some conservationists. And it must deal with certain theological items, for example, which suggest that God doesn't love little boys when they are naughty. Also, the print size and pictures must be substantially enlarged. These limited changes are now in hand.

These will be made available in whole or in part, up to grade 12, to all home school and home school centers as well as to private and public schools and to homes for supplementary education. Also included in the school package will be:

1. *Math It*, a simple, rapid-learn mathematics course for elementary (or any other) level for remedial or regular students, by E. H. Brooks, and proven in many schools and school system seminars as well as on television. This is an area which frustrates many parents, and teachers too. Students usually improve phenomenally in a few days. Even engineers and business men are using it.

2. Several series of books and tapes on Bible heroes and great characters of history.

3. Other sound and efficient books on spelling, handwriting, government, science, music, art. All will be a part of the "package," although parents or teachers need only select those parts which they want.

4. Educational toys, dolls, tools, etc. These are designed to carry out character-development ideals, stir the imagination, and provide a balance of hand with head and heart. Wherever practicable, these will be integrated with the McGuffey books. All royalties will go into Hewitt's home education program.

5. A brief simple "How to Teach" book for parents—and teachers.

Homes, or schools, or others interested in using these, or in selling them to others—for example, as a cottage-industry—may send a self-addressed stamped envelope to Hewitt Research Foundation, 36211 S.E. Sunset View, Washougal, WA 98671, for fuller information, which is being prepared as this book goes to press. These are already endorsed by educators, home-schoolers and church and family groups coast to coast and meet all standards for sound learning programs.

We are preparing these materials and programs—for home schools and as educational supplements for regular school children—on the basis of extensive research and more than thirty years of home schooling experience. But all of this genius is not ours, for we are constantly looking elsewhere too for sound creative ideas which meet the real needs of our children. And we are finding them—as, for example, Professor Brooks's *Math-It*, which receives high recommendations by university, public, and church school faculties.

We are also working to help other publishers to reshape their philosophies, goals, and programs in order to meet the unique needs of home schools. We send out basic information on our materials through our Parent-Educator and Family Report. A sample copy is available by sending a stamped self-addressed envelope to the Hewitt Research Foundation headquarters.

Just developed by Hewitt Child Development Center is a new curriculum designed for simple and effective teaching by parents and for supplemental and remedial education for all homes and schools. Information can be obtained by writing Hewitt Research Foundation at the address given above.

Appendix B

MICHIGAN V. O'GUIN

(A petition by the prosecuting attorney and the district judge which points out that the district court in Marquette, Michigan was not in their opinion the place to deal with a home school problem)

Comes now Dale Ruohomaki, Prosecuting Attorney for the County of Marquette, and moves for the entry of a Writ of Nolle Prosequi on the above charge for the following reasons:

1. Defendants were charged with Failure to Send Child To School.
2. Further investigation indicates that the offense is not motivated by criminal intent but rather by a good faith belief by the Defendants that their religious freedom is being infringed.
3. It appears that a legal rather than a factual question is presented, which in view of certain popular prejudices, should be decided in some manner other than a criminal trial by jury.
4. The remedy desired by the people is to have the legal question decided and the child returned to school, but the District Court lacks equitable powers and appears not to be the appropriate forum for the remedy sought.

WHEREFORE, IT IS PRAYED that a writ of Nolle Prosequi be entered.

Dated: 3/13/73 _____/signed/_____

Dale Ruohomaki, Prosecuting
Attorney

ORDER OF NOLLE PROSEQUI

To the Clerk:
Let an Order of Nolle Prosequi be entered.

Dated: March 13, 1973 _____/signed/_____

George E. Hill, District Judge

Appendix C

CALIFORNIA V. WILLIAMS

(Another case strongly stressing religious convictions in which the district attorney threw the case out of court for constitutional reasons)

STATEMENT OF FACTS

LARRY WILLIAMS and his wife, NELL WILLIAMS, reside at 424 Howell Mountain Road in the St. Helena School District. They have a child, aged seven, named GREGORY, that they have not and will not enroll in school as required by California Education Code Section 12101. Both Mr. and Mrs. Williams are members of the Seventh-day Adventist Church. Mr. Williams is employed as a professor at Pacific Union College, and Mrs. Williams is a housewife. The Williams base their refusal to have their child attend school on personal, moral, and religious convictions.

CYRUS PEARSON, employed as a guidance consultant by the Napa County Superintendent of Schools and as a child welfare and attendance officer of St. Helena School District, has carefully investigated the case and presented to this office a request for a Criminal Complaint requesting prosecution of the parents for their failure to send GREGORY to school. Pursuant to that request, a District Attorney's Citation Hearing was held on January 18, 1973, and there were in attendance both of the proposed defendants, Mrs. Alsman, a sister of Nell Williams, Chaplain W. B. Bristow, who is the Public Relations Director of the Northern California Conference of Seventh-day Adventists, and Claude D. Morgan, Esq., who is the attorney for the Northern California Conference of Seventh-day Adventists. At that hearing Mr. Pearson and this writer were satisfied that the problems relating to the Williams children, other than GRE-GORY, were satisfactorily resolved. The Williams, husband and wife, reiterated their refusal either to have GREGORY attend school or to fulfill the alternatives provided by law, such as a church school or tutor, again basing such refusal on moral and religious convictions. They contend that the provisions of the California law imposing criminal sanctions upon persons who refuse to send their children to school are an unconstitutional invasion of the free exercise of religious clause of the First Amendment of the United States Constitution made applicable to the States by the Fourteenth Amendment.

See also Article 1, Section 4 of California Constitution.

Chaplain Bristow explained briefly that the Seventh-day Adventist Church teaches its members, as a matter of religious conviction, that children should not be required to attend school until they were at least eight years of age, and possibly not until they were at least ten years of age. That as a part of his duties as Public Relations Officer of the Northern California Conference of Seventh-day Adventists, in each such case, he made inquiry as to the sincerity of the person urging this type of conviction, and that he had done so in this case. He further stated that he was satisfied, as a result of his investigation of the

148

Williams, that their beliefs were indeed sincere in their religious convictions, and that they were firmly held. He pointed out that many Seventh-day Adventists do not have such convictions, even though they were taught by the Church, and that the Church therefore would not support a person without such convictions. The Church, of course, imposes no discipline upon those who do not follow the conviction. They do support those who, like the Williams, they believe to have firm convictions. Both Chaplain Bristow and Mr. Morgan were asked to present materials in support of their position: Chaplain Bristow as to the religious conviction, and Mr. Morgan as to the law applicable to the case, so that we could study those materials to determine whether or not a Complaint should issue. Materials have been received and reviewed by the writer. Defendants rely principally upon *Wisconsin v. Yoder*, 92 S Ct. 1526. Chaplain Bristow has entered a book, entitled "Education", authored by Ellen G. White, copyright 1903, together with several extracts from that text, and other writings by the same author, the principal of which is attached hereto, marked Exhibit "A", and incorporated by reference herein. He also presented several scientific papers supporting from a scientific point of view the contentions of the Church that children should not attend school until they have attained a degree of maturity that one would not expect until the child was at least eight, or perhaps ten.

FACTUAL CONCLUSIONS

I have made the following conclusions of fact, and I would expect these facts to be found to be true after a full fair trial of the issues:

1. The defendants are the parents of a child of the age of seven years who is not attending school.

2. The parents' refusal is based upon sincerely held religious convictions.

3. The doctrine taught by the Church, as prepared by Mrs. White, is in fact a principal tenet of the Church that could be held by reason of the teachings of the Church as a firm moral conviction.

4. There is a great body of scientific evidence that supports the teachings of the Church.

5. It is my opinion that members of the Seventh-day Adventists' faith holding so strongly this moral conviction would never, in any event, send their children to public schools, but rather have them educated in the academies administered by the Church.

DISCUSSION

The principal case applicable here is *Wisconsin v. Yoder, supra.* In that case, members of the Old Order Amish Religion and the Conservative Amish Mennonite Church had refused to send their children to school beyond the eighth grade in contravention of the laws of Wisconsin requiring children to attend school until age sixteen. Parenthetically, I draw from the case, too, that Wisconsin's minimum age is seven, while Oregon's minimum age is eight. The Amish had based their refusal to require their children to attend school upon religious grounds, asserting that as to them Wisconsin's law was unconstitutional and unenforceable because it precluded their free exercise of religion. The Court in a very careful analysis appeared to be weighing the interest of the State in the education of the children as opposed to the right of the parents' free exercise of religion. A part of their analysis included the following language:

> "If it appears that parental decisions will jeopardize the health or safety of the child, or have a potential for significant social burden", the interests of the State will be paramount, otherwise the parents' rights should be paramount.

In that case, the Amish introduced evidence that their method of teaching children was equally as valid as the State's. That no jeopardy was attached to the safety or health of the children and clear and convincing proof that there was no potential for significant social burdens by reason of their free exercise of the Amish religion. The Supreme Court held that as to the Amish people Wisconsin's compulsory attendance law was unconstitutional. That case, of course, is on the opposite end of the age spectrum from our own.

Our case has another distinguishing feature. The Amish people unanimously held to the view that their children should not attend school beyond the eighth grade, as opposed to our case in which perhaps less than 25% of the Seventh-day Adventists believe that children should not attend school until they have reached sufficient maturity, that is, perhaps, between the ages of eight and ten. The draft evasion cases seem to me to be controlling, however, as to that issue. They are U.S. v. Seeger, 85 S Ct. 850, and Welsh v. U.S., 90 S Ct. 1792. In those cases the Court was considering the personal religious and moral beliefs of men who had refused induction, some of whom belonged to no organized religion and some of whom held these religious and moral convictions that were not necessary tenets of the faith that they professed. Welsh, for instance, was a Catholic; Seeger an agnostic. The church to which the others belonged is not stated. The Court, in those cases, was examining in essence the question of whether or not a person's personal religious and moral convictions were entitled to the same weight and dignity as those communally held by particular faiths and supported by some recognized church or religious organization. The Court, in analyzing this question as it applied to the draft laws, held that personal convictions, if they were based on moral and religious grounds, were entitled to equal dignity and protected by the free exercise of religion clause of the First Amendment to the Constitution of the United States.

CONCLUSIONS

It appears to this writer that absent some very strong proof that children's failure to attend school until they are at least eight years of age will jeopardize either the health or safety, mental or physical well-being of the child, or absent some strong proof that a child's failure to attend school until it has reached a sufficient maturity, that is, somewhere between the ages of eight and ten, would have a real and identifiable potential for significant social burdens, that a conviction of the Williams should not be had, and that if it were had on a trial level, would in all probability be reversed on appeal.

Respectfully submitted,

/signed/
_____

JOHN N. COOLEY
Assistant District Attorney

Appendix D

NEBRASKA V. RICE

(The findings in a Nebraska case which was won by the Rices but was appealed by the prosecutor to the state supreme court in which that court upheld the Rices' victory at the district level)

1. Courts: Juveniles: Appeal and Error. An appeal from the order of a county court sitting as a juvenile court to the District Court and to this court requires that we review the adjudication de novo on the record and reach an independent conclusion on disputed issues of fact.

2. Minors: Parent and Child: Statutes: Evidence. Whether a parent has neglected or refused to provide proper or necessary subsistence, education, or other care necessary for the health, morals, or well-being of a minor child under the provisions of section 43–202 (2) (c), R. R. S. 1943, is a question of fact, and each case must be determined on its own facts.

3. Minors: Parent and Child: Statutes: Schools and School Districts. Neglect of a parent to provide proper or necessary education for the health, morals, or well-being of a minor child under the provisions of section 43–202 (2) (c), R. R. S. 1943, is not proved by simply establishing that the compulsory school attendance law, section 79–201, R. R. S. 1943, has been violated.

Heard before Krivosha, C. J., Boslaugh, McCown, Clinton, Brodkey, White, and Hastings, J.

HASTINGS, J.

This is an appeal by the State of Nebraska from a judgment of the District Court reversing a finding by the county court of Lincoln County, sitting as a juvenile court, that Leslie Sue Rice, a minor, was a "child . . . whose parent . . . neglects or refuses to provide proper or necessary . . . education, or other care necessary for the health, morals, or well-being of such child," as provided for in section 43–202 (2) (c), R. R. S. 1943.

The dispositional hearing was held on December 1 and 2, 1977. At that time the minor was just past 13 years of age. She lived in Wallace, Nebraska, with her mother and father, and had completed the sixth grade in the Wallace public school system the preceding year. However, both she and her parents were what they denominated "born-again Christians," and as such, among other things, believed in a more or less literal and fundamental interpretation of the Bible; supported the view of creation and rejected totally the theory of evolution; and believed that the responsibility of all education of a child rested solely with the parents rather than the state. For some time they had been dissatisfied with the curriculum and textbooks of the public school system, primarily because they were not religiously oriented, and they had been searching for a satisfactory alternative. They became aware of and made inquiry to the Christian Liberty Academy of Prospect Heights, Illinois, which operated a

conventional religious primary and secondary school accredited by the state of
Illinois, as well as approximately 300 satellite schools consisting of 1,000 students scattered throughout the 50 states. As a result, the Rice Christian Academy was created, consisting of Lesley Rice, the minor's father, as headmaster;
Dixie Rice, the mother, as teacher; and, of course Leslie Sue as the only
student. A classroom was set up in the home, and textbooks, lesson plans,
reading lists, problems, and tests were furnished by the parent organization in
Prospect Heights, which offered needed consultation by telephone when required, and read and graded the various work papers and tests. There appeared
to be no question but what the minor attended seventh grade classes at the Rice
Christian Academy on a daily basis and during regular and conventional school
hours.

The mother had one semester of college, but possessed no teaching experience. Mr. Rice had engaged successfully in several of the building trades, was
currently well employed, and, in addition, he and his wife owned and operated
a hotel, a laundromat, and several rental properties. The academy was not
approved by the State of Nebraska, nor were the textbooks accepted for the
teaching of American history, as required by state law. Leslie Sue attended no
school during the 1977–78 school year other than Rice Christian Academy.

Other than the lack of official approval, the only criticism of the quality of
education offered by the Rice Christian Academy was by the Wallace superintendent of schools. He agreed that he had not spent enough time to make a
worthwhile overall evaluation. However, he questioned the history book as
being more of a summary than an in-depth investigation of American history,
and noted the apparent absence of courses of study in physical education and
health and safety. Other deficiencies pointed out by another witness related to
the absence of presentation of alternative philosophies and beliefs and of daily
interactions with peer groups.

On the other hand, an assistant professor of psychology from the University
of Nebraska at Omaha, after extensive testing of Leslie Sue and a comparison
with her tests from prior years while attending public schools, noted a general
deterioration of her relative achievement standing up through the testing in the
fall of 1977, but considerable progress from then until July of 1978, after her 1
year at the Rice Christian Academy. Based upon Leslie Sue's progress, as
revealed by the various tests, the witness ventured the opinion that her education was quite satisfactory.

Another witness who qualified as an expert in the field of education and
curriculum review testified that from his examination of the subjects taught at
Rice Christian Academy he found them to be comprehensive and adequate.

It is conceded by all parties concerned that the Rice Christian Academy is
not an approved school by state standards. Rule 14, Revised, of the Nebraska
State Department of Education, is the regulation and procedure for approving
the continued operation of all schools and the opening of new schools. It was
enacted pursuant to authority granted by the Legislature in section 79–328, R.
R. S. 1943. Rule 14-(0), General Provisions, thereof, provides in part: "Only
school systems approved for continued legal operation by the State Board of

Education was [sic] considered to be providing a program of instruction which is in compliance with the compulsory attendance laws." Rule 14 was properly introduced into evidence by the State at the hearing in the District Court.

An appeal from the order of a county court sitting as a juvenile court to the District Court and to this court requires that we review the adjudication de novo on the record and reach an independent conclusion on disputed issues of fact. §§ 43–202.03, 24–541, and 25–1925, R. R. S. 1943; *State v. Worrell*, 198 Neb. 507, 253 N. W. 2d 843 (1977). However, this court will give great weight to the findings of fact made by the trial court because it heard and observed the parties and the witnesses. *State v. Bailey*, 198 Neb. 604, 254 N. W. 2d 404 (1977). Whether a parent has neglected or refused to provide proper or necessary subsistence, education, or other care necessary for the health, morals, or well-being of a minor child under the provisions of section 43–202 (2) (c), R. R. S. 1943, is a question of fact, and each case must be determined on its own facts. *State v. Randall*, 187 Neb. 64, 187 N. W. 2d 586 (1971).

The State contends that the compulsory attendance laws as found in Chapter 79 of the Nebraska statutes, and Rule 14, *supra*, must be construed in pari materia with the juvenile court act, Chapter 43, article 2, including section 43–202 (2) (c), R. R. S. 1943, and that therefore the "proper or necessary . . . education . . . necessary for the health, morals, or well-being of such child" which must be provided by the parent is attendance at a school approved for compulsory attendance. In furtherance of its position, it points to section 79–211, R. R. S. 1943, which, after having provided for written warning to the person in charge of a child not attending school under section 79–201, R. R. S. 1943, requires that a complaint be filed in juvenile court, and section 79–216, R. R. S. 1943, mandates that anyone violating this act shall be guilty of a misdemeanor and be fined about $5 to $100, or be imprisoned in the county jail for not more than 90 days, or both.

Sections 79–201 and 79–211, R. R. S. 1943, were originally enacted in 1901, and have remained in more or less their present form. However, section 43–202 (2) (c), R. R. S. 1943, makes no reference to the proceeding mentioned in section 79–211, nor does section 43–202 (4) (b), which grants the juvenile court exclusive jurisdiction of a child "who is habitually truant from school or home; . . . ." The present-day language of section 43–202 (4) (b), R. R. S. 1943, was enacted in 1913, and then for the first time defined habitual truancy as an act of delinquency aimed at the child itself. Therefore, at Chapter 79, our laws proscribed the conduct of parents in not sending children to school, and section 43–202 (4) (b) accomplished the same purpose as to the child. This would seem to cover completely the subject of compulsory school attendance, but these laws were not invoked by the State in this case.

In 1955, the Legislature, in separating for definitional purposes a dependent and a neglected child, included the present-day language of section 43–202 (2) (c), R. R. S. 1943. This for the first time included the provision relating to the neglect or refusal of a parent to provide proper education "necessary for the health, morals, or well-being" of a child. It is obvious from an examination of that language that the legislative intent was to categorize children who were destitute or without home or support as neglected; those who were abandoned for practical purposes or were not receiving the proper kind of parental care as neglected; and those who were vicious or with criminal bent as delinquent. In 1973, the Legislature deleted the identifying names as "dependent," "neglected," or "delinquent," but the descriptions remain as subsection (1), subsection (2), and subsections (3) and (4), respectively, of section 43–202, R. R. S. 1943.

It is our opinion that Chapter 79, R. R. S. 1943, relating to compulsory school attendance, and section 43–202 (2) (c), R. R. S. 1943, regarding the neglect of children, generally do not pertain to the same subject matter and should not be construed in pari materia. *From v. Sutton,* 156 Neb. 411, 56 N. W. 2d 441 (1953). Additionally, the Legislature when enacting legislation is presumed to have knowledge of all previous legislation on the subject so that if it intended to equate nonattendance under Chapter 79 with "neglect" under section 43–202 (2) (c), R. R. S. 1943, it would have said so. *Bass v. County of Saline,* 171 Neb. 538, 106 N. W. 2d 860 (1960).

We feel that section 43–202 (2), including subsection (c), R. R. S. 1943, relates to actions by parents amounting to neglect, abandonment, or denial of proper care such as will endanger the health, morals, or well-being of a child. From our view of the evidence, such a situation does not exist here, and is not proved simply by establishing that the parents *may* be violating the compulsory school attendance law, which latter question we do not here decide.

The judgment of the District Court was correct and is affirmed.

AFFIRMED.

MICHIGAN V. WENBERG

(Summary of defense statements to appellate court after ad litem attorney appealed the decision favoring the defense.)

Erik Wenberg is not in a classroom because of the religious beliefs of the Wenbergs. The Wenbergs' religion teaches that a child should be taught at home with the mother as the teacher until the age of 8 to 10 years when a child has been taught how to differentiate between right and wrong, has developed his cause-to-effect reasoning to a higher degree and has developed his cognitive learning functions and until he is more mature physically. To read the Appellant's Brief one would assume that the Wenbergs wish to deny Erik an education completely. This is very much contrary to the facts. Erik's parents believe in education, are highly educated themselves and are very much concerned, in fact more so than most parents, with their son's education. The testimony at Trial showed that Erik is far advanced in many areas other than reading. Although he may be somewhat behind his age peers in reading development, that is not surprising since the Wenbergs have not emphasised that skill because of eye development. Dr. Moore indicated that that decision is based soundly in scientific study and that Erik will catch and pass his age peers.

All parties stipulated that the Wenbergs' beliefs are sincerely held. It then became the duty of the State to show that there was a paramount State interest not being satisfied and which could be satisfied in no other manner other than the manner prescribed, namely education with a structured routine. No such evidence was introduced. Erik will be going into a classroom sometime around the age of 8 to 10 years, and it is Dr. Moore's testimony that he will at that point be in a state of development wherein he can grasp the academic subjects easier and will have a better behavior and social quotient than his peers. Dr. Haynes testified that he knows of no scientific evidence why a child should be in school at age 6 but said it was a "convention of society." Dr. Moore also testified that he had done an extensive study into the Compulsory Education Laws of the 50 states and could find no scientific basis for putting children in school at the early age of six years.

The State of Michigan in its statutory scheme also recognizes that these early years in a classroom are not crucial. If a child lives beyond two and one-half miles from a public school, in the absence of bus transportation, he does not have to attend school until age nine. (MCLA 380.1561 (3) (c)) However, Appellees submit that Erik is in fact receiving an education at his home, pursuant to his parents' religious beliefs, that is surpassing that of his age peers. He is verbally very fluent, his conceptual abilities are well developed, his fund of common knowledge is advanced for a child his age. The State has not met its burden of proof under *Yoder, Meyer, Pierce, Nobel* or any of the other cases and shown that there is a compelling State interest that is not being satisfied. All of the cases dealing with early childhood home education which has been quoted or cited from in either Appellant's or Appellee's Briefs, have been decided in favor of the home education because the State has been unable to show that there is a compelling State interest in having a child in a classroom when the parents can do as good a job at home pursuant to their religious beliefs.

The Trial Judge made a correct finding that Erik has not been harmed in any way, and that therefore, the Court is unable to interfere with the free exercise of the Wenbergs' religious beliefs.

RELIEF REQUESTED

The Appellees request that the Judgment of the Trial Court be affirmed.

Dated: October 6, 1981   Respectfully submitted,

STATE OF MICHIGAN

IN THE CIRCUIT COURT FOR THE COUNTY OF OAKLAND

IN THE MATTER OF ERIC W.

Proceedings had before the Honorable JOHN N. O'BRIEN, Circuit Judge, in the Courthouse in the City of Pontiac, Oakland County, Michigan, on Thursday, October 29, 1981.

APPEARANCES:
Mr. Kingsley Cotton, appearing
    for Appellant
Mr. Vernon L. Alger, appearing
    for Appellee

Sheila Steinhoff,
RO194
Official Court Reporter

Sixth Judicial Circuit
October 29, 1981

RULING OF THE COURT, ONLY:
THE COURT: I don't know if it's digressing or not, but I wonder if you gentlemen have ever heard it expressed that Benjamin Franklin was sent home from school at about the eighth grade with a note to his mother indicating that he was uneducatable, true, a hyperactive child. I suppose the only reason I say that, and whether that is true or not we don't know.

MR. ALGER: I understand the same thing is also true of Thomas Edison.

THE COURT: Maybe I'm mixing up my heroes, but at any rate, the only reason I mention that is that it all does become somewhat relative.

The statute involved requires that a parent provide care for a child and specifically, as we get to the circumstance that is involved in this case, education as required by law.

The Probate Court as the trial Court, the Court below in this particular instance, held that there must be a showing of sufficiently measurable harm before that Court is going to conclude neglect.

I think with that position the Appellant has generally disagreed.

The statute requires, that is the Court below felt that the statute requires there be a finding of neglect or refusing to provide education as required by law, and then the Court below went on to apply that as required by law, not in its literal sense, but in its qualified sense, in that it, the Court, had an obligation, when that—as required by law—is challenged by the right to religious freedom as protected by the State and Federal Constitution, to measure to what degree, required by law, can interfere with the exercise of that religious freedom.

This phrase, required by law, the Court felt necessitates a measurement of the degree of invasion into what I think you have referred to as the parents' authentic, sincerely held religious belief, that is consistent with the Seventh Day Adventist Church.

For the purpose of seeing if the invasion into that constitutionally protected religious freedom could be tolerated in this particular case.

I haven't heard any argument here and the Court does not believe that generally the State cannot limit the religious beliefs. However it's equally true that generally the State, and when I say the State, the Government, can limit the exercise of religion. However, the Courts have, I think, been consistent in finding that the limitation that the State chooses to impose or is permitted to impose in the exercise of religion, not its beliefs, will be tolerated or exist when that exercise of religion interferes with some serious societal interests.

The Court below in this case found as insufficient, the measurement, the measurement that there was an educational lagging. The Court found it insufficient to justify an invasion by the State into a sincerely held authentic religious belief and the practice of the parents in connection with the Seventh Day Adventist Church.

I think that the Court below reviewed the testimony and test results that were submitted and found that there was not such a potential for or actuality of harm to justify society invading this authentic, sincerely held religious practice.

This Court disagrees with Appellant's conclusion that the mere existence of the statute which requires education, and a showing that the statute is not being followed, that that automatically results in a finding of neglect, where there is asserted, responsibly asserted, as a cause for not following the statute, the constitutionally protected right to the freedom of the exercise of religious beliefs.

Accordingly this Court affirms the Court below in its conclusions.

Thank you, gentlemen, for a most interesting case.

CERTIFICATION

STATE OF MICHIGAN   )
                             :SS
COUNTY OF OAKLAND)

I, SHEILA STEINHOFF, Official Court Reporter for the Circuit Court of the County of Oakland, HEREBY CERTIFY that the foregoing transcript is a true and correct transcription of my stenotype notes taken in said case on the date indicated.

_____/signed/_____

SHEILA STEINHOFF
Official Court Reporter
Sixth Judicial Circuit
Oakland County, Michigan

DATED: 10–30–81

GEORGIA V. BLANKENSHIP

(A trial brief presented by attorneys before the trial of a single mother who won in an Atlanta, Georgia, trial.)

Defendant, Patty Blankenship, operates a fundamental, Bible-believing and teaching home located in Georgia. Defendant is a believer who holds a firm conviction that the Bible is the inspired Word of God and that it must serve as the source of guidance for all aspects of life.

The operation of Defendant's School is centered on the biblical concepts that all men are sinners, that the consequence of sin is eternal separation from God in a literal hell, that this consequence can be avoided only in one way, by trusting in Jesus Christ alone for one's salvation, and the fact of His death, burial and resurrection as a payment for all sins for those who will believe.

Among the biblical mandates addressed to the Defendant is the command to give one's children a Christian education. Proverbs 22:6 states, "Train up a child in the way he should go. . . ." This verse requires that Christian parents educate their children according to God's Word, in a manner consistent with the teachings of the Bible. Faced with this command the Defendant believed that the only way to fulfill that command would be to establish her own school where her children could learn in a Christian environment. As a result of this conviction, Defendant's School began operation in the fall of 1979.

The Defendant's School differs from other educational methods in that all subjects are presented to the students from a biblical viewpoint, so that in each subject taken by the student he is constantly learning to embody within himself the Christian way of life. Thus, the curriculum used in Defendant's School is replete with verses taken directly from the Bible. A child working in reading, therefore, will learn to read by reciting Bible verses and at the same time the verse will reflect on an ideal Christian character trait which the child should emulate. A child learning via this system, therefore, is continuously being exposed to the Word of God, no matter what may be the subject he is presently studying. As such all subjects taught as part of the curriculum are religious in nature, not secular.

At the present time, there are approximately 3500 unapproved Christian schools operating throughout the United States, with about 800 more scheduled to begin operation in 1980. A number of unapproved Christian schools are now operated in Georgia of which Defendant's School is one. Test results of Defendant's School show that an education is being received in the basic subjects that is equal, if not superior, to the education being received by the students in the Georgia public schools.

No application has ever been made by or on behalf of Defendant's School to the State Department of Education of the State of Georgia for approval of Defendant's School as an approved school system. The Defendant does not hold a teaching certificate or permit issued by the State Department of Education of the State of Georgia.

The defense would also submit that the Supreme Court of the United States has already addressed the issue of the religious nature of subjects taught in denominational schools and has held that secular subjects taught in those schools are still sufficiently religious in influence so as to warrant First Amendment protection. Every Christian school case that has been ruled on by the Supreme Court of the United States has found that Christian education is a religious activity protected by the First Amendment. For example, in *Lemon v. Kurtzman*, 403 U.S. 602, 609 (1970) we find that:

> Although the court found that concern for religious values does not necessarily affect the content of secular subjects, it is also found that the parochial school system was "an integral part of the religious mission of the Catholic Church."

Justice Douglas in his concurring opinion stated it as follows:

> The analysis of the constitutional objections to these two state systems of grants to parochial or sectarian schools must start with the admitted and obvious fact that the *raison d'etre* of parochial schools is the propagation of a religious faith. *Id.* at 628.

And in *Meek v. Pittinger*, 421 U.S. 349, 366 (1975) the Court stated that:

> The very purpose of many of those schools is to provide an integrated secular and religious education; the teaching process is, to a large extent, devoted to the inculcation of religious values and belief.

Because of the religious influence in the teaching of secular subjects, the court found that it could not approve funding even of secular instruction in private Christian schools. The conclusion must be drawn, then, that if the education of students by these private Christian schools is so religious so as to violate the establishment clause if public funds are used, then this religious nature of the schools is also entitled to the protection guaranteed religion by the free exercise clause. As such, any limitation of free exercise may be permitted only if there is a compelling state interest.

The defense believes that this testimony and case-law is sufficient proof that all instruction at Defendant's School is religious in nature and biblically based. Every subject taught at Defendant's School involves religious instruction. Therefore, Defendant properly should be exempt from the general school laws of Georgia including state approval.

LAW

THE GEORGIA EDUCATIONAL STATUTES AS WELL AS THE RULES PROMULGATED BY THE GEORGIA STATE DEPARTMENT OF EDUCATION VIOLATE THE INDIVIDUAL PARENT'S FUNDAMENTAL

RIGHTS TO BEAR, RAISE AND EDUCATE HER CHILDREN AS PRO-
VIDED FOR UNDER THE NINTH AND FOURTEENTH AMENDMENTS
TO THE UNITED STATES CONSTITUTION.

The statutes, insofar as the Defendant is not in compliance with them, are
unconstitutional in that they violate the Defendant's fundamental right to
bear, raise and educate her children as she sees fit. It will be noted that the
above-mentioned rights are not specifically enumerated in the United States
Constitution, but this does not mean that they do not exist. These rights have
been long recognized by legal scholars and by the Courts as not only existing
but as being fundamental. Many legal scholars have found them in the phrase
"liberty" of the Fourteenth Amendment which reads in part that no one "shall
be deprived of life, liberty or property without due process of law." Others have
pointed to the Ninth Amendment to the U.S. Constitution as the source of
these fundamental rights:

> The enumeration in the constitution, of certain rights, shall not be construed to deny
> or disparage others retained by the people.

Whatever the source of these rights may be, they have long been recognized
by the American Courts and by freedom-loving people everywhere as a cor-
nerstone of American liberty. The United Nations Declaration of Human
Rights recognizes that the fundamental unit of society is the family, and that
parents have a right to control the education of their children.

These fundamental rights are clearly recognized by the Supreme Court of
Minnesota in *Thiede v. Town of Scandia Valley*, 14 N.W.2d 400 (1944):

> The entire social and political structure of America rests upon the cornerstone that all
> men have certain rights which are inherent and inalienable. Among these are the right
> to be protected in life, liberty, and the pursuit of happiness; the right to acquire,
> possess, and enjoy property; and the right to establish a home and family rela-
> tions . . . , at 405.

Similarly, in U.S. Supreme Court cases, the right of privacy within marriage
or family, including the right to have children, has long been recognized, but
increasingly so in recent years, as evidenced by *Carey v. Population Services
Intern.*, 431 U.S. 816, 97 S.Ct. 2010, (1977); *Roe v. Wade*, 410 U.S. 113, 93
S.Ct. 705, (1973); *Griswold v. State of Connecticut*, 381 U.S. 479, 85 S.Ct.
1678 (1965).

These principles have long been recognized by the United States Supreme
Court specifically as applied to education. *Meyer v. State of Nebraska* 262 U.S.
390, 43 S.Ct. 625 (1923). *Meyer v. State of Nebraska* involved a Nebraska law
which prohibited the teaching of foreign languages before a certain age level.
The Court in this case quoted the Fourteenth Amendment provisions concerning "life, liberty or property" and went on to state:

> While this court has not attempted to define with exactness the liberty thus guaran-
> teed, the term has received much consideration and some of the included things have

been definitely stated. Without doubt, it denotes not only freedom from bodily restraint, but also the right of the individual to contract, to engage in any of the common occupations of life, to acquire useful knowledge, to marry, establish a home and bring up children, to worship God according to the dictates of his own conscience, and generally to enjoy those privileges long recognized at common law as essential to the orderly pursuit of happiness by free men., at 399.

The Court continued by pointing out the right of the teacher to teach, and the right of a parent to engage a person to teach, thus indicating the right of parents to choose the type of education their children should receive:

Plaintiff in error talked this language in school as part of his occupation. His right thus to teach and the right of parents to engage him so to instruct their children, we think, are within the liberty of the amendment., at 400.

See also *Bartels v. State of Iowa,* and *Bohning v. State of Ohio,* both cited at 262 U.S. 404, 43 S.Ct. 628 (1923), two cases decided at the same time as *Meyer v. Nebraska, supra,* involving the teaching of German, and decided in accordance with the principles stated in *Meyer v. Nebraska.*

The right of parents to control and decide their children's education is a clearly recognized fundamental constitutional right. As such, it may not be unduly interfered with by the State. What constitutes a legitimate reason for such interference: Here the courts have become much more restrictive in recent years. In earlier decisions, such as *Pierce* and *Meyer, supra,* the standard seemed to be that the regulation which infringed upon parental rights must bear a reasonable relation or a substantial relation to a legitimate state purpose. But that has changed. The burden on the State is now a much greater one. Under recent cases previously cited, such as *Roe v. Wade, supra,* the standard must now be "compelling state interest." The State may not simply employ a "balancing act," that is balancing the state interest against the degree of interference with parental right. Rather, the State interest must be "compelling" or the parental right to educate the child must be held inviolate.

Is there then a "compelling state interest" in education of children? It should be noted first that the state has no federal constitutional mandate that requires the state to maintain the public school system. As stated by the Supreme Court of the United States in *San Antonio Independent School District v. Rodriguez,* 411 U.S. 1, 93 S.Ct. 1278 (1973):

Education, of course, is not among the rights afforded explicit protection under our Federal Constitution. Nor do we find any basis for saying it is implicitly so protected. . . . , at 35.

We have carefully considered each of the arguments supportive of the District Court's finding that education is a fundamental right or liberty and have found those arguments unpersuasive., at 37.

See also *Goss v. Lopez,* 419 U.S. 565 (1975).

However, the fact that public education is not constitutionally mandated does not necessarily establish that the state has no compelling interest in the education of the young. Nor does the Defendant feel constrained, in order to support her position to maintain that the state has no such compelling interest. However, that compelling State interest, if it exists at all, must be carefully defined as to its true nature. In *Commonwealth v. Roberts*, 159 Mass. 372, 34 N.E. 402 (1893), the Supreme Court of Massachusetts stated concerning compulsory education statutes:

> The great object of these provisions of the statutes has been that all children shall be educated, not that they shall be educated in any particular way.

And as the U.S. Supreme Court observed in *Wisconsin v. Yoder*, 406 U.S. 205, 92 S.Ct. 1526, 32 L.Ed.2d 15 at 92 S.Ct. 1539:

> We should also note that compulsory education and child labor laws find their historical origin in common humanitarian instincts, and that the age limits of both laws have been coordinated to achieve their related objectives. In the context of this case, such considerations, if anything, support rather than detract from respondents' position. The origins of the requirement for school attendance to age 16, an age falling after the completion of high school, are not entirely clear. But to some extent, such laws reflected the movement to prohibit most child labor under age 16 that culminated in the provisions of the Federal Fair Labor Standards Act of 1938. It is true, then, that the 16-year child labor age limit may to some degree derive from a contemporary impression that children should be in school until that age. But at the same time, it cannot be denied that, conversely, the 16-year education limit reflects, in substantial measure, the concern that children under that age not be employed under conditions hazardous to their health, or in work that should be performed by adults., at 227–228.
>
> The requirement of compulsory schooling to age 16 must therefore be viewed as aimed not merely as providing educational opportunities for children, but as an alternative to the equally undesirable consequence of unhealthful child labor displacing adult workers, or, on the other hand, forced idleness. The two kinds of statutes— compulsory school attendance and child labor laws—tend to keep children of certain ages off the labor market and in school; this regimen in turn provides opportunity to prepare for a livelihood of higher order than children could pursue without education and protects their health in adolescence., 228.

But to sustain the constitutionality of the compulsory attendance laws as found in the Georgia Educational Statutes and Rules, the State must do more than show that it has a "compelling state interest."

As the U.S. Supreme Court stated in *United States v. Robel*, 389 U.S. 258, 88 S.Ct. 419 (1967), the case involving the Subversive Activities Control Act which prohibits a Communist from employment in a defense plant but which included persons actually engaged in subversive activity and others who were not actually engaged in subversive activity:

> It has become axiomatic that *precision* of the regulation *must be the touchstone* in an area so closely touching our most precious freedoms. Emphasis added, at 265.

The Court referred to other cases supporting this position: *NAACP v. Button*, 371 U.S. 415, 438, 83 S.Ct. 328, 340, 9 L.Ed.2d 405 (1963); *Aptheker v.*

Secretary of State, 378 U.S. 500, 512 through 513, 84 S.Ct. 1659, 1667, 12 L.Ed.2d 992; *Shelton v. Tucker*, 362 U.S. 479, 488, 81 S.Ct. 247, 252, 5 L.Ed.2d 231 (1960). The Court in *Robel* concluded by saying:

> We are concerned solely with determining whether the statute before us has exceeded the bounds imposed by the Constitution when First Amendment rights are at stake. . . . Our decision today simply recognizes that, when legitimate legislative concerns are expressed in a statute which imposes a substantial burden on protected First Amendment activities, Congress must achieve its goal by means which have a 'less drastic' impact on the continued vitality of First Amendment freedoms. . . . The Constitution and the basic position of First Amendment rights in our democratic fabric demands nothing less., at 267.

Similarly, in *Cleveland Board of Education v. LaFleur*, 414 U.S. 643, 94 S.Ct. 791 (1974), the Supreme Court decided the case involving a school board policy of mandatory termination dates for teachers who become pregnant. The State attempted to uphold such statutes for said policies by pointing to the need for continuity of teaching, and by pointing out that teachers beyond a certain stage of pregnancy are no longer competent to teach. LaFleur argued that this mandatory cut off date was unconstitutionally unfair because some women teachers could work beyond said mandatory cut off date. The Court agreed:

> While the medical experts in these differed on many points, they unanimously agreed on one—the ability of any particular pregnant woman to continue to work past any fixed time in her pregnancy is very much an individual matter. Even assuming, arguendo, that there are some women who would be physically unable to work past the particular cut-off dates embodied in the challenged rules, it is evident that there are large numbers of teachers who are fully capable of continuing work for longer than the Cleveland and Chesterfield County regulations will allow. Thus, the conclusive presumption embodied in the rules, like that in *Vlandis*, is neither "necessarily [nor] universally true," and is violative of the Due Process Clause.," at 646–647.

In *LaFleur*, the Court referred to a case involving a similar issue, *Stanley v. Illinois*, 405 U.S. 645, 92 S.Ct. 1208, 31 L.Ed.2d 551, in which the State of Illinois had adopted a statute which contained an irrebuttable presumption that unmarried fathers are incompetent to raise their children. The Supreme Court in *Stanley* held:

> It may be, as the State insists, that most unmarried fathers are unsuitable and neglectful parents. It may also be that Stanley is such a parent and that his children should be placed in other hands. But all unmarried fathers are not in this category; some are wholly suited to have custody of their children., at 654.

Because the Court held that this irrebuttable presumption unfairly violated the rights of Stanley since the State could have employed a less drastic means of deciding such cases on individualized basis, the Court struck down the Illinois statute as violative of due process.

Another similar case was *Vlandis v. Kline*, 412 U.S. 441, 446, 93 S.Ct. 2030, 2233, 37 L.Ed.2d 63. *Vlandis* involved a Connecticut statute which established an irrebuttable presumption that non-residency for the purpose of qualifying for reduced tuition rates at a State University, saying that "permanent irrebuttable presumptions have long been disfavored under the Due Process Clauses of the Fifth and Fourteenth Amendments," the Court held:

> . . . it is forbidden by the Due Process Clause to deny an individual the resident rates on the basis of a permanent and irrebuttable presumption of non-residence, when that presumption is not necessarily or universally true in fact, and when the State has reasonable alternative means of making the crucial determination., at 452.

What do the residency requirements, teacher pregnancy termination dates, and unmarried fathers, have to do with compulsory education laws? Simply this: they all involve an irrebuttable presumption. The compulsory education statute, if so construed to deny the Defendant the right to have her children taught [at] home violates the Defendant's fundamental constitutional right to control the direction of children, by creating an irrebuttable presumption that she, being an uncertified teacher and not a college graduate, is not competent to teach children. Paraphrasing the Court in *Stanley*, we can say that many, possibly even most, persons who are not certified teachers are not capable of supplying the educational needs of children, but it is certainly not true that all persons so uncertified are so uncompetent. Many persons are very capable of teaching children effectively, even though they may not be certified. Furthermore, it is also well known that there are public school teachers who are certified but who are not competent to teach children effectively. As the Franklin County Franklin Circuit Court, Division One, observed in *Reverend C. C. Hinton, Jr., et al. v. Kentucky State Board of Education, et al.*, Civil Action No. 88314, filed October 4, 1978:

> Expert testimony in this case certainly established that there is not the slightest connection between teacher certification and enhanced educational quality in state private schools. *U.S. v. Seiger*, 380 U.S. 163; *U.S. v. Ballard*, 322 U.S. 78.

The *Hinton* case, similar to the instant case, involved a group of parents who were charged with truancy for sending their children to a church-related school which did not meet state approval. Basing its decision largely on First Amendment rights rather than rights of parental authority, the Trial Court concluded that the State has no controlling State interest in enforcing State standards upon private schools, except for health, fire and safety standards. This decision was appealed to the State Supreme Court and affirmed. *Kentucky State Board of Education v. Rudasill*, 26 K.L.S. 13, rendered 10/10/79, 589 S.W.2d 877 (1979).

The question must be asked to them, "what compelling state interest" is there in taking Defendant's children out of their private home school and forcing them into the mediocrity of public education? The State, *Hinton* to the contrary, may possibly have a compelling state interest in insuring that Defendant's children receive a quality education. However, it is clearly possible that their children could receive a quality education without being compelled to attend a public school or a private school at which teachers are required to be certified. Further, as to the State's "compelling interest" in insuring that children are not subject to child labor, idleness and crime, this clearly is not a legitimate concern with the Defendant's children.

The Defendant concludes, then, that any statute which does not allow parents to educate their children through schools established in their own home is unconstitutional as applied to the Defendant. As the Court observed in *Roberts, supra:*

> Without doubt, then, the Massachusetts compulsory attendance statute might well be constitutionally infirm if it did not exempt students whose parents prefer alternative forms of education. And as to the scope of alternatives permitted by our statute, our Supreme Judicial Court has construed the "otherwise instructed" statutory exemption to include home education, given by the parents themselves, "provided it is given in good faith, and is sufficient in extent." *Commonwealth v. Roberts,* 159 Mass. 372 at 374.

The State, then, must allow church schooling, at least in cases where the parents are providing a quality education, or its statutes will not survive constitutional attack. The State could provide, for example, that schooling will be evaluated on an individual case-by-case basis or by standardized testing.

The State might possibly object that this would be a costly and improper burden. The Defendant answers by pointing to the Court in *Stanley, supra,* which stated:

> The Constitution recognizes higher values than speed and efficiency; the Bill of Rights in general, and the due process clause in particular, were designed to protect the fragile values of the vulnerable citizenry from the overbearing concern for efficiency and efficacy which may characterize praiseworthy government officials no less, and perhaps more, than mediocre ones.

LAW

THE STATE'S CASE SHOULD BE DISMISSED SINCE THE APPLICATION OF THE GEORGIA SCHOOL LAWS AND REGULATIONS TO DEFENDANT'S SCHOOL VIOLATES DEFENDANT'S RIGHT TO THE FREE EXERCISE OF RELIGION AS GUARANTEED BY THE FIRST AND FOURTEENTH AMENDMENTS TO THE UNITED STATES CONSTITUTION.

Defendant's School receives no financial aid from State or Federal agencies to assist it in its operation.

The law of multiple jurisdictions is clear and unambiguous that for purposes of legal consideration a school may be considered as an integral and inseparable part of a church. *Westbury Hebrew Congregation, Inc. v. Downer,* 59 Misc.2d 387, 302 N.Y.S.2d 923 (1969); *What Constitutes "Church," "Religious Use"* or the Like Within Zoning Ordinances, 62 A.L.R.3d 197 (1975); *Diocese of*

Rochester v. Planning Board, 1 N.Y.2d 508, 136 N.E.2d 827 (1956). *Catholic Bishop of Chicago v. Kinger*, 371 Ill. 257, 20 N.E.2d (1939).

> Religious use is not defined solely in terms of religious worship. Clearly, it extends to *education* which is offered by a religious institution primarily for the children of its members. It clearly includes the church itself, a *parochial school* with its normal components for recreational and other extracurricular activity. . . (emphasis added). *American Law of Zoning* 2d Vol. 1 Section 12.25 at p. 459 and 460.

As stated with quoted mention and approval in the decision of *Diocese of Rochester et al. v. Planning Board of Town of Brighton et al.*:

> A church is more than merely an edifice affording people the opportunity to worship God. Strictly religious uses and activities are more than prayer and sacrifice and all churches recognize that the area of their responsibility is broader than leading the congregation in prayer. . . . To limit a church to being merely a house of prayer and sacrifice would, in a large degree, be depriving the church of the opportunity of enlarging, perpetuating and strengthening itself and the congregation. . . ." 1 N.Y.2d 445, 136 N.E.2d (1956).

In *City of Concord v. New Testament Baptist Church*, 382 A.2d 377 (1977), the court ruled that a special zoning permit was not needed to operate a day school ministry of the New Testament Baptist Church. According to the court the school "was a permitted use under the ordinance allowing facilities usually connected with a church." A "school may be considered as an integral and inseparable part of a church."

The proposed use of an estate as a religious education center by the Protestant Episcopal Church was held to come within a town zoning ordinance permitting a "church or similar place of worship" in residential districts. The buildings on the property consisted of a main residence house, a tenant house, a boathouse, and a barn. The Church planned to conduct there, for adults and selected teen-aged youths, a series of programs of supervised religious study, seminars, contemplation, and training with emphasis on Christian living and service. *Diocese of Central New York v. Schwarzer*, 23 Misc.2d 515 199 N.Y.S.2d 939, aff'd 13 App.Div.2d 863, 217 N.Y.S.2d 567 (1960).

Since Defendant's School is inseparably a part of Defendant's faith, any attempt by the State of Georgia to regulate or control the functions of the School could involve a violation of the free exercise rights of the Defendant. Defendant's opposition to state approval is based on a theological conviction that the State cannot control or dictate to an entity that belongs to God. State approval of her home-religious school would therefore be in violent opposition to the convictions of the Defendant.

It is the theological conviction of the Defendant which distinguishes their situation from that of other Christian schools which have accepted state approval. The people who operate those schools have accepted state approval because they have not been hindered from so doing by any theological conviction. They have been willing to accept state approval as a precondition to operating. Rev. Levi Whisner, pastor of God's Tabernacle and Tabernacle Christian School, had a similar struggle with the School authorities in Ohio, wherein the State had attempted to claim a right to approve his Christian School, which also utilized a Christian education program. Reverend Whisner's position was that any attempt by the State to require his Christian school to conform to the same rules and regulations followed by the public school would directly violate his individual religious conviction and unduly burden his free exercise of religion. The Supreme Court of Ohio agreed, holding that the "minimum standards" for public and non-public schools as promulgated by the State Board of Education constituted an infringement upon Reverend Whisner's constitutional right to the free exercise of religion. *State v. Whisner,* 47 O.S.2d 181, at 204, 351 N.E.2d 750 (1976). As a matter of convictional belief, therefore, Defendant cannot in good faith allow the State to approve, accredit or regulate in any way her School, since that would be equivalent to the approval, accreditation, or regulation of her faith.

The State would imply the Defendant's attitude as one of disregard for the legislative and judicial processes of Georgia, implying that Defendant considers herself above the law. In reality, the Defendant is asserting a right guaranteed her by the First Amendment of the United States Constitution, the right to the free exercise of her religion. Refusing State approval of her School, thereby subjecting herself to criminal and civil prosecution, is the only way that the Defendant can effectively preserve the rights guaranteed her under the First Amendment. In addressing itself to issues of free exercise, the Supreme Court of the United States has never expressed disapproval of those people who take a firm stand based upon their truly-held religious convictions. On the contrary, the Court has impliedly bestowed its imprimatur upon such stances as the only viable method of voicing First Amendment freedoms:

> The impact of the compulsory-attendance law on respondents' practice of the Amish religion is not only severe, but inescapable, for the Wisconsin law affirmatively compels them, under threat of criminal sanction, to perform acts undeniably at odds with fundamental tenets of their religious beliefs. *Wisconsin v. Yoder,* 406 U.S. 205, at 218 (1972).

Nowhere in the *Yoder* case will one find a reprimand by the Court to the Respondents for refusing to comply with Wisconsin's compulsory attendance law based upon their religious convictions. Thus, the State can hardly label as a disregard for the law Defendant's present stance toward Georgia school laws.

Since the contention that State approval and regulation of Defendant's School impinges upon the rights of Defendant to the free exercise of her religion, it is incumbent upon the State to prove that such approval or regulation is necessary to satisfy a compelling state interest. The defense would submit that the only interest the State has in this area is to insure that children receive a solid education in the basic subjects. This interest has been satisfied in the case of children attending Defendant's School. The defense will now elaborate on the law which supports its position.

IN RESOLVING THIS CASE, THIS COURT MUST APPLY THE CON-
STITUTIONAL STANDARD ENUNCIATED IN *WISCONSIN V. YODER.*

A.   The Requirement, That The Defendants Prove That The Georgia Statutes And Regulations Constitute An Arbitrary And Unconstitutional Exercise Of The State Police Power, Has Been Supplanted
By *Yoder*, Which Places The Burden Of Proof On The State To Show
That The Statutes And Regulations Serve A Compelling State Interest Which Could Not Otherwise Be Served By Some Means Having A Less Drastic Impact On The Free Exercise Of Defendant's
Religion.

The constitutional test for the validity of statutes which allegedly infringe on
religious rights has changed dramatically in recent years. The early cases employed a standard which placed the burden of proof on the Plaintiffs to prove
that the state statutes and regulations were arbitrary, unreasonable, and irrelevant to the legitimate state interest in educating its citizens. See *Meyerkorth v.
State*, 115 N.W.2d 585 (1962) at 590, 596. In *Sherbert v. Verner*, 374 U.S. 398
(1963), the Supreme Court applied a constitutional standard which requires
the Defendants to show that the state statute imposes a burden on the free
exercise of religion. 374 U.S. at 970. By making this allegation in the instant
case, the Defendant has made out a prima facie case sufficient to shift the
burden of proof to the State. Under *Sherbert*, once the Defendant has made a
showing that the statute burdens the free exercise of her religion, the burden of
proof then shifts to the state to show that some *compelling state interest* justifies
the infringement of Defendant's First Amendment right. 374 U.S. at 406.

It is basic that no showing merely of a rational relationship to some colorable state
interest would suffice; in this highly sensitive constitutional area, "[o]nly the gravest
abuses, endangering paramount interests, give occasion for permissible limitation." *Id.*
(quoting *Thomas v. Collins*, 323 U.S. 516, 530).

Furthermore, "it would plainly be incumbent upon [the State] to demonstrate that no alternative forms of regulation would [further the compelling
state interest] without infringing First Amendment rights." *Id.* at 407. *Sherbert*
is the foundation of the modern constitutional standard.

In *Wisconsin v. Yoder*, 406 U.S. 205 (1972), the Court reiterated the constitutional standard of *Sherbert*. First, it looked to the issue of whether the
compulsory education law of Wisconsin tended to infringe on the free exercise
of the Amish faith. It held:

The conclusion is inescapable that secondary schooling, by exposing Amish children
to worldly influences in terms of attitudes, goals and values contrary to beliefs, and by
substantially interfering with the religious development of the Amish child and his
integration into the way of life of the Amish faith community at the crucial adolescent
stage of development, contravenes the basic religious tenets and practice of the Amish
faith, both as to the parent and child.

The impact of the compulsory-attendance law on respondents' practice of the Amish religion is not only severe, but inescapable, for theWisconsin law affirmatively compels them, under threat of criminal sanction, to perform acts undeniably at odds with fundamental tenets of their religious beliefs. *Id.* at 218.

In the instant case, the Defendant alleges that the School provides an education which is centered upon the principle that all knowledge flows from the Bible; that as a matter of firmly-held religious conviction, a parent enrolls her child at the School so that the child may be trained to lead a good, Christian life; that the laws and regulations of the State of Georgia interfere with the free exercise of these religious convictions. These allegations satisfy the *Sherbert-Yoder* constitutional standard.

Finding that the Wisconsin law constituted an infringement on the practice of the Amish religion, the Court in *Yoder* then applied the second tier of the *Sherbert* test. First, the State urged that it had power to regulate conduct, so long as it did not interfere with freedom of conscience. The court rejected this argument, holding that:

". . . to agree that religiously grounded conduct must often be subject to the broad police power of the State is not to deny that there are areas of conduct protected by the Free Exercise Clause of the First Amendment and thus beyond the power of the State to control, even under regulations of general applicability." *Id.* at 220 (citing *Sherbert v. Verner*, 374 U.S. 398 [1963]).

The state then contended that the compulsory education statute was not intended to interfere with religious activity, and was facially neutral; the Court held that "[a] regulation neutral on its face may, in its application, nonetheless offend the constitutional requirement for government neutrality if it unduly burdens the free exercise of religion." *Id.* (citing *Sherbert v. Verner, supra*).

The court then applied the "compelling state interest" test set forth in *Sherbert:*

We turn, then, to the State's broader contention that its interest in its system of compulsory education is so compelling that even the established religious practices of the Amish must give way. Where fundamental claims of religious freedom are at stake, however, we cannot accept such a sweeping claim; *despite its admitted validity in the generality of case we must searchingly examine the interests that the State seeks to promote by its requirement for compulsory education at age 16, and the impediment to those objectives that would flow from recognizing the claimed Amish exemption. Id.* at 221 (emphasis added).

Two legitimate state interests underlying the compulsory education law were acknowledged by the Court: preparation of citizens to participate intelligently in the political system, and preparation of individuals to be self-reliant participants in society. *Id.* The Court then balanced these state interests against the First Amendment claims of Jonas Yoder. The standard enunciated required that the state interest be compelling, and that the state employ a means of furthering that interest having the least drastic impact on respondents' Free Exercise rights:

The essence of all that has been said and written on the subject is that only those interests of the highest order and those not otherwise served can overbalance legitimate claims to the free exercise of religion. We can accept it as settled, therefore, that, however strong the state's interest in universal compulsory education, it is by no means absolute to the exclusion or subordination of all other interests. *Id.* at 215 (citing *Sherbert v. Verner, supra*).

The Court, in applying the *Sherbert* test, concluded that the Amish had carried their initial burden of proving the sincerity of their religious convictions, and that the State regulatory scheme infringed upon those beliefs. Having made this showing, "it was incumbent on the State to show with more particularity how its admittedly strong interest in compulsory education would be adversely affected by granting an exemption to the Amish." *Id.* at 236. Because the State had failed to meet this burden, the Court held the Wisconsin compulsory education statute unconstitutional as applied.

There can be no doubt that *Sherbert* and *Yoder* articulate the proper standard for determining the constitutionality of the regulatory scheme at issue in the instant case.

Pierce v. Society of Sisters, 268 U.S. 510 (1925), was an early United States Supreme Court case which held that an Oregon statute requiring all school age children to attend public schools constituted an arbitrary exercise of the state police power. *Pierce* was given an expansive construction by the United States Supreme Court in *Yoder*, where the Court held that *Pierce* stands for the proposition that:

. . . the values of parental direction of the religious upbringing and education of their children in their early and formative years have a high place in our society. . . . Thus, a state's interest in universal education, however highly we rank it, is not totally free from a balancing process when it impinges on fundamental rights and interests, such as those specifically protected by the Free Exercise Clause of the First Amendment, and the traditional interest of parents with respect to the religious upbringing of their children so long as they, in the words of *Pierce*, "prepare [them] for additional obligations." 402 U.S. at 213–214.

B.　An Examination Of The Modern Case Law, Consistent With Georgia's Position in the Instant Case, Shows That Those States Have Abandoned The Legal Premises Upon Which The Prosecution Depends.

A recent Ohio decision is very instructive in the instant case, *State of Ohio v. Whisner*, 47 Ohio St.2d 181, 351 N.E.2d 750 (1976). In *Whisner*, the Ohio Supreme Court held that the application of the compulsory education law, in conjunction with the "minimum standards" for Ohio elementary schools, was unconstitutional as applied to parents who wished to send their children to a Christian school whose curriculum was premised on the Christian truth that all knowledge flows from the Bible, and that the salvation of man depends upon accepting God as the ultimate source of truth, and accepting Jesus Christ as

Savior. *Id.* at 199–200. The state standards in *Whisner*, as in the present case, were "so pervasive and all-encompassing that total compliance with each and every standard by a non-public school would effectively eradicate the distinction between public and non-public education, and thereby deprive these appellants of their traditional interest as parents to direct the upbringing and education of their children." *Id.* at 211–12.

The *Whisner* court properly applied the standard of review enunciated in *Sherbert* and *Yoder*, looking first to whether the parents' religious beliefs were truly-held religious convictions, and then to whether the state regulation of their school (albeit neutral on its face) infringed the free exercise of those religious beliefs. Finding that the Ohio "minimum standards" had the effect of "obliterat[ing] the 'philosophy' of the school and impos[ing] that of the state," *id.*, at 216, the burden then shifted to the state to show some compelling state interest which was served by application of the "minimum standards" to the Tabernacle Christian School which could not be otherwise served by some less drastic form of state action. *Id.* at 217–18. Because the record was void of any such evidence, the *Whisner* court held that the Ohio minimum standards were unconstitutional as applied to parents who enrolled their children at Tabernacle Christian School.

Special deference is given to the right of parents to govern the religious upbringing of their children in a New Hampshire decision rendered in January 1978. In *City of Concord v. New Testament Baptist Church*, 382 A.2d 377 (1978), the Supreme Court of New Hampshire decided a case which involved the issue of "whether a five-day-a-week school run by a fundamentalist church is a facility 'usually connected with a church.'" *Id.* at 378. The court held:

> The tenets of faith and beliefs of the members of the New Testament Baptist Church require as a convictional matter that their children receive a Bible-oriented education every day of the week, not just on Sunday morning. . . .
>   The congregation believed as a matter of conviction, not just convenience, the school must open despite lack of approval from all civil authorities. . . .
>   . . . [T]he parents and members of the congregation believe as a matter of religious conviction that their children should not be taught secular humanism in the public schools but receive a Christian education. As in *Yoder*, "they object to [public] education generally, because the values [it] teaches are in marked variance with [their] values and . . . way of life." *Id.* at 378–79 (quoting *Wisconsin v. Yoder*, 406 U.S. at 210–11).

After examining the long history of religious involvement in education in the United States, the court concluded:

> Thus a school may be considered as an integral and inseparable part of a church. *Id.* at 380.

In 1964, the Supreme Court of California decided *People v. Woody*, 40 Cal.Rptr. 69, 394 P.2d 813 (1964). The court held that a statute prohibiting the use of peyote (a mild hallucinogen), was unconstitutional as applied to adherents of the Native American Church, an Indian religious sect which employed the drug as part of its religious ceremony. The court applied the constitutional standard of review enunciated in *Sherbert v. Verner* (*Yoder* had not yet been decided), determining "first, whether the application of the statute imposes any burden upon the free exercise of the defendants' religion, and second, if it does, whether some compelling state interest justifies the infringement." 394 P. 2d at 816. Because the use of peyote was an integral and inseparable aspect of the Native American faith, state prohibition of its use had an obvious deleterious effect on the defendants' religion. *Id.* at 818. The court then addressed the compelling state interests which were proffered by the State.

The state contended that the use of peyote would have a detrimental effect on the Indian community and that a religiously-based exception to the prohibition against the use of peyote would lead to fraudulent claims of an asserted religious use of the substance. *Id.* The former contention was dismissed on the ground that the record did not support the state's contentions that the drug was harmful, or that it might lead to the use of other drugs, or that it might be consumed by children. *Id.* To the Attorney General's argument that the use of peyote "obstructs enlightenment and shackles the Indian to primitive conditions," the court held:

> We know of no doctrine that the state, in its asserted omniscience, should undertake to deny to defendants the observance of their religion in order to free them from the suppositious "shackles" of their "unenlightened" and "primitive condition." *Id.*

Addressing the state's contention that a religiously based exemption from the criminal statute would lead to fraudulent claims, the court held that *Sherbert* required the state to offer some sort of proof that such fraudulent claims were likely; moreover, "'it would plainly be incumbent upon the [state] to demonstrate that no alternative forms of regulation would combat such abuses without infringing First Amendment rights.'" *Id.* at 819 (quoting *Sherbert v. Verner*, 374 U.S. at 407).

Because the State had failed to meet its burden of proof, the court ruled that the criminal law prohibiting the use of peyote, though facially valid, was unconstitutional as applied to members of the Native American Church. *Id.* at 821–22.

Another noteworthy aspect of *Woody* is that the court took into consideration the fact that members of the Native American Church observe higher moral standards than do Indians outside the church. *Id.* at 88. In *Wisconsin v. Yoder*, the Supreme Court made the following observation regarding the Amish community:

> Its members are productive and very law-abiding members of society; they reject public welfare in any of its usual modern forms. . . .
> There can be no assumption that today's majority is "right" and the Amish and others like them are "wrong." A way of life that is odd or even erratic but interferes with no rights or interests of others is not to be condemned because it is different.
> . . . .
> There is nothing in this record to suggest that the Amish qualities of reliability, self-

reliance, and dedication to work would fail to find ready markets in today's society. 406 U.S. at 222–24.

It is uncontroverted that the Defendant's School trains its students to employ the Bible as their guide in life; that its students are taught to observe higher moral standards than are students in the public schools; that the educational program instills in its students qualities of independence and self-reliance; that its students are trained to be patriotic and law-abiding; that the Defendant receives no State or Federal aid, nor would she seek such aid.

The protections afforded defendants under the Free Exercise Clause of the First Amendment have been made applicable to the states through the Fourteenth Amendment. *Cantwell v. Connecticut*, 310 U.S. 296, 303 (1940). *Wisconsin v. Yoder* is the authoritative interpretation of the Free Exercise Clause, which governs the instant case. Under *Wisconsin v. Yoder*, the Defendants are required to demonstrate that their religious convictions are truly held, and that their religious faith and their mode of life are inseparable and interdependent. 406 U.S. at 215, 235. Defendant must then demonstrate that the state program of regulating her Christian school has a detrimental impact on the free exercise of their religious convictions. *Id.* at 217–18, 235.

C.   The Religious Beliefs Of Defendant Are Truly Held; She Has Chosen To Educate Her Children In A Christian School Because Her Firmly Held Religious Convictions Mandate That Her Children Be Taught According To The Biblical Truth That All Knowledge Flows From God.

The Defendant follows essentially the teachings of the Bible as a matter of firm convictional belief and incorporates the Bible and its principles into every aspect of her daily life. Defendant believes that she must raise and educate her children only in the Christian way of life as prescribed in the Bible. It is her belief that such education must be divorced from any and all influences or philosophies which are not totally Bible-centered. Since the philosophy of the public schools and the State Department of Education obviously is not, and cannot be, biblically centered, Defendant believes that any action by the State Department of Education in approving or regulating her school would be equivalent to accepting the principles and philosophies of the public educational system, which would violate her own religious beliefs.

D.   The Georgia Education Regulatory Plan Is An Unreasonable, Pervasive And All-Encompassing Program Which, When Applied To Defendant, Denies Her The Free Exercise Of Her Religion.

Defendant has established her school because of her firm conviction that a Christian education which entails a complete Biblical Christian philosophy is essential to the salvation of her children. Under *Pierce v. Society of Sisters, supra,* a parent has a constitutional right to direct the religious and educational upbringing of his child. The Georgia compulsory education statutes require every parent to place his or her school-age children in regular attendance at a public, private, denominational, or parochial day school.

Taken together, these statutes infringe on the right of Defendant to freely exercise her religious beliefs. The regulatory plan which is imposed upon Christian schools has the effect of displacing the Biblically mandated religious and educational mission of the schools, and substituting a state-imposed philosophy of education which utterly ignores the Christian truths that the Bible is the ultimate source of knowledge, that acceptance of Jesus Christ as Savior is the only means of salvation, and that Christians should lead lives which adhere to the Word of God as it is reflected in the Bible. The multitude of regulations have the effect of standardizing all schools in Georgia, thereby obliterating the distinction between a Christian school and a public school. In *State v. Whisner,* 47 Ohio St.2d 181 (1976), the Supreme Court of Ohio held that the state "minimum standards" for elementary schools which had been promulgated by the State Board of Education violated the free exercise rights of parents who enrolled their children at Tabernacle Christian School, which was operated by a fundamentalist church. The court held:

> In our view, these standards are so pervasive and all-encompassing that total compliance with each and every standard by a non-public school would effectively eradicate the distinction between public and non-public education, and thereby deprive these appellants of their traditional interest as parents to direct the upbringing and education of their children. *Id.* at 211–12.

The constitutional rights of parents to direct the spiritual and educational growth of their children were upheld in *Pierce v. Society of the Sisters* and *Wisconsin v. Yoder.* Inasmuch as the Massachusetts regulatory program virtually dictates every detail of education, it has the effect of supplanting the First Amendment right of parents to provide their children a Christian education.

E.   The State Has Failed to Show That the Georgia Education Regulatory Plan Serves A Compelling State Interest Which Could Not Otherwise Be Served By A Means Having A Less Drastic Impact on Defendant's Right To Freely Exercise Her Religion.

It is incumbent on the state to show that its regulatory plan serves a compelling state interest, and that this interest could not be served by an alternative means having a less drastic impact on petitioners' free exercise rights. In *Yoder,* the Court held:

> The essence of all that has been said and written on the subject is that only those interests of the highest order and not otherwise served can overbalance legitimate claims to the free exercise of religion. We can accept it as settled, therefore, that,

however strong the State's interest in universal compulsory education, it is by no means absolute to the exclusion or subordination of all other interests. 406 U.S. at 215.

In *Sherbert v. Verner*, the Court held that once the citizen has shown that state action infringed upon the free exercise of her truly-held religious convictions, the burden of proof shifted to the State "to demonstrate that no alternative forms of regulation would [further the state interest] without infringing First Amendment rights." 374 U.S. at 407.

The state interest in education is rather narrow. *Yoder* held that "some degree of education is necessary to prepare citizens to participate effectively and intelligently in our political system . . ." and that "education prepares individuals to be self-reliant and self-sufficient participants in society." 406 U.S. at 221. The Nebraska Supreme Court was more explicit, when it held:

The state should control the education of its citizens far enough to see that it is given in the language of their country, and to insure that they understand the nature of the government under which they live, and are competent to take part in it. Further than this, education should be left to the fullest freedom of the individual. *Nebraska District of Evangelical Lutheran Synod of Missouri, Ohio, and Other States v. McKelvie*, 104 Neb. 93, 175 N.W. 531.

The state interest in education is fully satisfied, if students attending Christian schools learn to read, write, work with numbers, and understand the American form of government. It is submitted that students attending Defendant's School are actually more proficient in these skills than are children attending public schools. This fact, standing alone, fully satisfies the state interest in compulsory education. The *means* by which these results are obtained—whether "approved" by the state or not—are irrelevant to the state interest.

It is submitted that the least drastic means of satisfying the state interest in education would be through standardized testing, which focuses upon the results Christian schools obtain, rather than through pervasive regulation of the means by which the results are reached. Of course, such standardized testing should be gauged according to the results which are obtained in the public schools. Through this testing process, the state can fully satisfy its compelling interest in compulsory education, while making the least drastic imposition on the Defendant's free exercise rights. The State has not utilized this less-restrictive alternative method.

Under the test advanced in *Yoder* and *Sherbert*, the state has utterly failed to show why the state interest in education cannot be served by standardized testing, which would have the least drastic impact on Defendant's First Amendment rights. Although decided primarily on State Constitutional grounds, the Defendants attach the recent case of *Kentucky State Board for Elementary and Secondary Education (substituted as Defendant for Kentucky State Board of Education) an Administrative Board of the Commonwealth of Kentucky, et al., v. Reverend C. Harry Rudasill, et al.*, decided by the Kentucky Supreme

Court. The Court concludes that Certification of teacher and/or the approval of schools is not synonymous with a quality education.

CONCLUSION

The Defendant believes, as a matter of firm convictional belief, that the salvation of her children depends on their accepting the Bible as the divine and inerrant Word of God, and the ultimate source of all knowledge, and on accepting Jesus Christ as their personal Savior. She has created a Christian school, for the purpose of indoctrinating her children to base their lives upon the Bible, as well as to educate her children so that they may function effectively in society. The all-encompassing and detailed statutes and regulations of the State of Georgia are unconstitutional as applied to Defendant's school, because they are so pervasive that they displace the Biblical philosophy of the schools with that of the state. By governing every detail of the educational process, the State suffocates the Bible-based program which is employed by Defendant under course requirements, teacher certificates, policy statements, attendance records, and a multitude of other forms of bureaucratic red tape.

Because the regulatory program interferes with the free exercise of Defendant's truly-held religious convictions, the State has the burden of proving that the plan furthers a compelling state interest. Under the decisions of various jurisdictions and United States Supreme Court, the state interest in education is to guarantee that children become proficient in reading, writing and arithmetic, and be able to understand the American governmental system. This compelling interest must be served by the means having the least drastic impact on the free exercise of Defendant's religion. It is uncontroverted that the education which Defendant's children receive at her school is at least as good as that which is offered in public schools, and that the results obtained in Christian schools fully satisfy the state's interest in education. The state could fully satisfy its interest by monitoring the actual results which are being generated in Christian schools through standardized testing of all schools. Standardized testing insures that the State's compelling interest in education is satisfied, and has the least drastic impact on the free exercise of Defendant's religion.

Respectfully submitted,
GIBBS & CRAZE

by: _____

Charles E. Craze
Attorney for Defendants
6929 West 130th Street
Suite 600
Parma Heights, Ohio 44130
(216)845-6800

Appendix G

CIVIL RIGHTS

42 U.S. CODE

§ 1983. Civil action for deprivation of rights

Every person who, under color of any statute, ordinance, regulation, custom, or usage, of any State or Territory or the District of Columbia, subjects, or causes to be subjected, any citizen of the United States or other person within the jurisdiction thereof to the deprivation of any rights, privileges, or immunities secured by the Constitution and laws, shall be liable to the party injured in an action at law, suit in equity, or other proper proceeding for redress. For the purposes of this section, any Act of Congress applicable exclusively to the District of Columbia shall be considered to be a statute of the District of Columbia.

R.S. § 1979; Pub.L. 96–170, §1, Dec. 29, 1979, 93 Stat. 1284.

§ 1985. Conspiracy to interfere with civil rights

Preventing officer from performing duties

(1) If two or more persons in any State or Territory conspire to prevent, by force, intimidation, or threat, any person from accepting or holding any office, trust, or place of confidence under the United States, or from discharging any duties thereof; or to induce by like means any officer of the United States to leave any State, district, or place, where his duties as an officer are required to be performed, or to injure him in his person or property on account of his lawful discharge of the duties of his office, or while engaged in the lawful discharge thereof, or to injure his property so as to molest, interrupt, hinder, or impede him in the discharge of his official duties;

Obstructing justice; intimidating party, witness, or juror

(2) If two or more persons in any State or Territory conspire to deter, by force, intimidation, or threat, any party or witness in any court of the United States from attending such court, or from testifying to any matter pending therein, freely, fully, and truthfully, or to injure such party or witness in his person or property on account of his having so attended or testified, or to influence the verdict, presentment, or indictment of any grand or petit juror in any such court, or to injure such juror in his person or property on account of any verdict, presentment, or indictment lawfully assented to by him, or of his being or having been such juror; or if two or more persons conspire for the purpose of impeding, hindering, obstructing, or defeating, in any manner, the due course of justice in any State or Territory, with intent to deny to any citizen the equal protection of the laws, or to injure him or his property for lawfully

179

enforcing, or attempting to enforce, the right of any person, or class of persons, to the equal protection of the laws;

Depriving persons of rights or privileges

(3) If two or more persons in any State or Territory conspire or go in disguise on the highway or on the premises of another, for the purpose of depriving, either directly or indirectly, any person or class of persons of the equal protection of the laws, or of equal privileges and immunities under the laws; or for the purpose of preventing or hindering the constituted authorities of any State or Territory from giving or securing to all persons without such State or Territory the equal protection of the laws; or if two or more persons conspire to prevent by force, intimidation, or threat, any citizen who is lawfully entitled to vote, from giving his support or advocacy in a legal manner, toward or in favor of the election of any lawfully qualified person as an elector for President or Vice President, or as a Member of Congress of the United States; or to injure any citizen in person or property on account of such support or advocacy; in any case of conspiracy set forth in this section, if one or more persons engaged therein do, or cause to be done, any act in furtherance of the object of such conspiracy, whereby another is injured in his person or property, or deprived of having and exercising any right or privilege of a citizen of the United States, the party so injured or deprived may have an action for the recovery of damages occasioned by such injury or deprivation, against any one or more of the conspirators.

R.S. § 1980.

§ 1986. Action for neglect to prevent

Every person who, having knowledge that any of the wrongs conspired to be done, and mentioned in section 1985 of this title, are about to be committed, and having power to prevent or aid in preventing the commission of the same, neglects or refuses so to do, if such wrongful act be committed, shall be liable to the party injured, or his legal representatives, for all damages caused by such wrongful act, which such person by reasonable diligence could have prevented; and such damages may be recovered in an action on the case; and any number of persons guilty of such wrongful neglect or refusal may be joined as defendants in the action; and if the death of any party be caused by any such wrongful act and neglect, the legal representatives of the deceased shall have such action therefor, and may recover not exceeding $5,000 damages therein, for the benefit of the widow of the deceased, if there be one, and if there be no widow, then for the benefit of the next of kin of the deceased. But no action under the provisions of this section shall be sustained which is not commenced within one year after the cause of action has accrued.

R.S. § 1981.

§ 1988. Proceedings in vindication of civil rights; attorney's fees

The jurisdiction in civil and criminal matters conferred on the district courts by the provisions of this Title, and of Title "CIVIL RIGHTS," and of Title

"CRIMES," for the protection of all persons shall be exercised and enforced in conformity with the laws of the United States, so far as such laws are suitable to carry the same into effect; but in all cases where they are not adapted to the object, or are deficient in the provisions necessary to furnish suitable remedies and punish offenses against law, the common law, as modified and changed by the constitution and statutes of the State wherein the court having jurisdiction of such civil or criminal cause is held, so far as the same is not inconsistent with the Constitution and laws of the United States, shall be extended to and govern the said courts in the trial and disposition of the cause, and, if it is of a criminal nature, in the infliction of punishment on the party found guilty. In any action or proceeding to enforce a provision of sections 1981, 1982, 1983, 1985, and 1986 of this title, title IX of Public Law 92–318, or title VI of the Civil Rights Act of 1964, the court, in its discretion, may allow the prevailing party, other than the United States, a reasonable attorney's fee as part of the costs.

R.S. § 722; Pub.L. 94–559, § 2, Oct. 19, 1976, 90 Stat. 2641; Pub.L. 96–481, Title II, § 205(c), Oct. 21, 1980, 94 Stat. 2330.